SERIOUSLY FUNNY

Life, Love and God . . . musings between
two good friends

Adrian Plass and
Jeff Lucas

Authentic

Reprinted 2010 (4), 2011, 2012

18 17 16 15 14 13 12   13 12 11 10 9 8 7

First published 2010 by Authentic Media
52 Presley Way, Crownhill, Milton Keynes, MK8 0ES
www.authenticmedia.co.uk

British Library Cataloguing in Publication Data

A catalogue record for this book is available from the British Library

978-1-85078-869-0

Cover Design by David Smart
Printed and bound by CPI Group (UK) Ltd., Croydon, CR0 4YY

SERIOUSLY FUNNY

Introduction: Adrian

When Jeff and I met to discuss the publication of our correspondence, we discovered a mutual fear. Briefly, it is this. The truth may well set us free, but it could also get us burned as heretics – in a metaphorical sense, I hasten to add. The thing about letters between friends is that there are no rules apart from those actually or implicitly agreed by the writers. We have explored what we think and feel and believe and don't believe in a way that might not be appropriate or even helpful in the context of formal ministry. Sometimes, though, you have to machete your way through the forest of this weary, wonderful world in order to find the path you should have been on in the first place. For me (for both of us, I think) this sweaty, arboreal process has been very helpful, and sometimes quite distressing. I have mentioned elsewhere an American author's comment that writing is easy, you just sit down at your typewriter and open a vein. That is not invariably true for me, thank the Lord, but it would be hard to find a better way to describe the painful process by which one or two of these messages from the heart have finally emerged.

Having said all this, readers will search this book in vain for dramatically bizarre heresies. We are not advocating

human sacrifice as a normal activity during church week-
ends, nor do we make a plea for greater tolerance of those
who wish to express themselves through the medium of
mutual disembowelment. Rather, they will find evidence
of a spiritually eccentric struggle towards understanding
the sanity, the humour, the compassion and the creative
ingenuity of a God who is frequently and disastrously categorised as narrow, simplistic, humourless and, frankly,
boring.

I have laughed a lot over Jeff's letters, not least because
they include accounts of excruciatingly embarrassing
moments. Equally importantly, I have wept a little and
learned a lot. How could I not, when again and again I
have caught a reassuring glimpse of the sad but smiling
face of Jesus?

Come and join us. Eavesdropping is allowed. You are
very welcome.

Introduction: Jeff

It was a whispered idea shared over a dinner table. Adrian and I were attending one of those Christian events that was so utterly boring, it seemed that the evening was designed for the cure of chronic insomniacs. As we looked around the room at the narrowed eyes and slumped shoulders of an audience who were desperately trying to fight off sleep during a numbing speech, designed to crash The Samaritans switchboard, we both felt that it might be useful to talk. But there was a double challenge in that. First of all, we are both manically busy, and were fearful that the next time we were together in the flesh (I hesitate to use that term as it always makes me feel like a naturist) might well be one of our funerals, during which conversational opportunities between us would be *so* limited, due to one of us being enclosed in a pine box. (Make mine oak. Pine is *so* eighties).

The other problem is that if Christians talk too loud, especially about delicate matters of faith, there are some self appointed thought police types who will rush in, lights flashing and sirens blaring, to arrest the unfortunate chatty soul and charge them with heresy and promptly set them ablaze. The smell of burning flesh has never been that attractive to me, especially when it's my own, and this fear does therefore tend to inhibit open conversation. Sadly, this means that many of us are trapped inside our own heads, locked up with some difficult fears, doubts and theories, but unable to air them in the sunshine with anyone else. That all becomes rather claustrophobic and, after a while, the walls of your head start to close in, squeezing your faith into a shrinking parcel. Spend too long like that, and one starts to fantasise about starting an escape committee to flee the cult. When the church becomes Colditz and the sentries have machine guns and fish badges on their armoured personnel carriers, it's time to dig a tunnel.

So Adrian and I decided to exchange letters. This in itself carries its own risks, as he is such a brilliant writer and, while I want him to look good, for him to look so good that I appear like a village idiot by comparison would not be helpful. There have been moments when his brilliance with words has made me feel like a yokel, but I don't mind. I've known for years that Adrian is a warm, kind, frustrated, happy, sad, hopeful bloke, and this exchange has been fun, therapeutic and distinctly unpressurised. We've been able to air our washing, but we haven't then had to iron it into neatness and create razor sharp creases.

So welcome to our chatter. We're glad you pulled up a chair.

ONE

Dear Jeff,

A memory has surfaced. It was something that happened to me twenty years ago, and I want to share the story with someone. I think you might understand. You always aim for the truth, despite being a Christian. I also want to tell you about a fascinating encounter I had just a few weeks ago with a Christian speaker who claimed to have lost his faith. The two stories go together in a way. Well, I think they do. You may not agree. I'll start with the memory.

Next to the new supermarket in our town there's a public house called The Bandolier, a family-owned, attractively uneven building, probably dating from late Victorian times. Over the last two decades quite a lot of changes have been made to the interior, but twenty years ago there were three bars. The saloon bar, traditionally a smarter, less turbulent environment in English pubs, was separated or perhaps buffered from the public bar by a small off-licence section staffed by a teddy bear-shaped, balding man, who concluded every transaction with the inexplicable words, 'Nice one, chief.' The significantly less smart public bar was a place where darts, bar billiards and dominoes could be enjoyed. This part of the pub became quite loud and rumbustious at times, albeit usually in a good-humoured sort of way. The third bar, the important one in my story, was called the snug. It was small, comfortable and generally very quiet, a plumpy armchair of a room, and an excellent home from home for people like me who enjoyed sitting in a corner with a good book and a pint of Harvey's bitter beer, a quaffing ale brewed by human beings, but designed and created by God himself.

So, there I luxuriated one early evening in October, sitting by a small table in the corner of the snug appreciating the healing power of the peace, the quality of the beer, the pungency of the season and the masterful construction of G K Chesterton's *The Honour of Israel Gow*, my favourite Father Brown story.

The only other people in the bar were two rather scruffy elderly men (not at all like me, a scruffy middle-aged man). As far as beer was concerned, I was a sipper and a relisher at the time, but these two were drinking for England. They were committed gluggers and downers, and the more golden amber they poured down their necks, the more they argued. It got worse and worse, louder and louder, less and less coherent. Fists were banged on tables, chairs were scraped back, until eventually the healthily beer-tinged atmosphere turned blue with oaths and curses as the two protagonists rose on unsteady legs to continue their disagreement at a higher plane.

Cue the landlord.

This impressively large-girthed, authoritative fellow had been running the pub for years. Tom was genial and accommodating to all his customers, but bad behaviour was not tolerated. Trouble makers got thrown out. It was as simple as that. He and I had chatted briefly on a few occasions. During that part of our lives Bridget and I (give our love to Kay, by the way) were appearing almost every night in an epilogue television programme called *Join the Company*. Broadcast in the south of England in the days before all-night television, it was the final item before the little white receding dot that hardly anyone remembers nowadays. It featured a group of four or five people, mainly Christians, sitting around a table discussing love, death, sex, war, finance, bereavement and other issues easily resolved in a space of no more than ten minutes. Because it was on so late, our audience tended to consist of insomniacs, taxi drivers, people who'd been watching snooker and not got round to turning their sets off yet, amused university students, policemen, night watchmen, depressives and, of course, publicans. I knew the land-lord of The Bandolier must have watched this more or less Christian programme quite often after clearing up in the evening, because he had referred to my involvement from time to time.

Tom came crashing through to the snug with a no-nonsense expression printed heavily on his large features.

'Oy, you two!' he thundered. 'There's no swearing in my pub! Out! Now!'

Then, to my inexpressible horror, he thrust a ham-like hand out in my direction and, as if in final justification of his action, uttered the following dismally memorable words:

'There's a religious gentleman sitting in the corner. Out!'

There was no arguing with such a force. After a brief Laurel and Hardy moment in the doorway, the miscreants shuffled out into the crisp autumn air, still mithering fiercely at each other. Tom, signalling the end of the affair with a decisive nod and a slap of both hands on the counter, returned to his duties in the public bar. I was left in wretched solitude. My volume of short stories lay unread. My pint of Harvey's stood untasted.

I was a religious gentleman sitting in the corner. I was part of the reason why people were liable to be thrown out of the pub for swearing. No doubt Tom would have taken the same action if I hadn't been there, but I could feel my cheeks flaming at the very notion that my 'religiousness' might be regarded as nothing but a negative motivation for pagans to mind their p's and q's. So much for proactive Christianity, eh? Those two old fellows who'd drunk more than was good for them had been cast into outer darkness, while I remained in the warm snug with my beer and my book. I remember joking once about an Irish Christian, who smuggled Bibles out of China, marvelling that the border guards miraculously never seemed to see them, but in a way the same thing had happened with me in The Bandolier. Gospel living turned inside out. Jesus goes to the pub and the locals get summarily ejected. Oh dear . . .

The thing is, Jeff, on that day, although I may have overreacted to a particular event, some kind of seed was planted in my understanding or my spirit or wherever it is that these seeds get planted. It was the seed of a decision that, metaphorically and in any other necessary way, I wasn't going to end up as a religious gentleman in the corner. The church does enough of that sort of thing without me adding to the problem. I hope that you and I will visit many a pub in the future, but let's not be religious, let's only be as gentlemanly as Jesus, and let's invite as many people as possible to join us in our corner. What do you think?

The second, more recent story.

A man rang me one day. I had never met him and his name was unfamiliar, but he told me that he had been a

Christian speaker and evangelist for some years after being converted from Islam.

'The thing is,' he said, 'I've lost my faith. I just don't believe in any of that stuff any more. God isn't just round the corner. He doesn't intervene in our lives, and all the things I've said to people over the years are a load of nonsense. I wondered if you and I could meet and talk about what's happened to me.'

I agreed a little nervously, and we met at one of my favourite places to eat or have coffee, a little café near the Lanes in Brighton. My new friend (I'll call him Ted) went through all the things he had said on the phone plus a lot more, sounding quite emphatic and final about his loss of belief in the very existence of God. Meanwhile, as is my wont on such occasions, I was screaming to God in my head, asking him to give me something dynamic and useful to say.

Nothing! Where is God when you need him? I just did lots of nodding and sympathetic murmuring and clicking of the tongue and all the other things that take the place of sanity in these situations. After an hour or so of Ted's explanations and my inane sound effects, my companion moved seamlessly into a description of the times when he had felt really close to God, and how much those times had meant to him. Slightly bewildered by this unexpected change of direction, I still had very little to say other than the aforementioned murmuring and clicking, although I have to add that I did incorporate some interestingly expressive nods as well.

As we parted a little later, Ted said, 'I want to thank you for what you've said this morning. I found it ever so helpful. '

I stared at him for a moment, trying to look like someone who had said something useful. I doubt if I succeeded.

'Ah,' I replied, 'that's good. Good! That's – that's really good.'

Later, on the train back to Polegate, I asked myself what had been going on with Ted. If I was a certain kind of Christian I would tell you that God answered that question for me. Perhaps he did. I don't know. The answer to my question, Jeff, wherever it came from, was that Ted had not lost his faith. He had lost everything except his faith.

By that I mean that he had again lost his faith in the god who stands behind our shoulders like a divine Jeeves, waiting to attend to any little needs or deficiencies in our lives, and is often dismissed when something goes drastically, terribly wrong or he fails to come up with the goods. The god who is intimately involved with fiddly details of our mortgages but, for some inexplicable reason, never challenges our incessant, blinkered greed. The tired, tedious, diluted, western god who saves a parking space for Mrs. Blenkinsop from the Abundant Living Church of Final Revelation when she does her shopping, but can't save a starving child from dying on the streets of a Bangladesh slum. And why not? Because there are not enough Christians who are willing to give themselves or their money or their time to be his hands and feet in the places where he longs to love the ones who need him most.

Aslan is on the move, they say. Is he? Is he really? Does he spend most of his time standing in supermarket parking spaces going 'Grrrrrh!' at any car that doesn't have a fish sticker attached to its boot? You know what this is, don't you, Jeff? This is the *Deal or no Deal* god, the one who looks a bit like a rejuvenated Noel Edmonds, presiding over a world where coincidences are regarded as amazing and significant when they happen, and conveniently ignored when they don't.

Ted had been confronted with the actual substance of his faith. I think he has to face up, as we all do at one time or another, to the fact that authentic faith survives because and despite, not just because. It might make us cry and rage, but it has to be confronted. Peter had to face it with Jesus. It nearly broke him to pieces. How hard it is to push on through our childish misconceptions of God to a place where we enjoy or fear or wrestle with a childlike awareness that our task is to believe in him and love him, and, dare I say it, praise him whatever happens or does not happen. Tough, isn't it? Tough, tough, tough. You might be there already, but I'm not.

So, those are my two stories, Jeff. And here's a question. If we two gentlemen were pushed into a corner and forced to be absolutely straight about our religion, what kind of truth would emerge, and would it set us free? I think it might. I hope so. We could at least have a go, couldn't we? Over to you.

      Love,
         Adrian

TWO

Dear Adrian,

How lovely to hear from you. I too am a fan (perhaps even a worshipper) of that beautiful beer you mentioned. Perhaps the ancient Hebrew word manna should be translated into the English 'Harvey's Sussex Bitter'. This is probably heretical nonsense, however, as the Israelites got bored with manna. The cosmos would implode before any human being could ever tire of quaffing the epic Sussex draft.

I was intrigued to hear about the pair of boisterous elderly chaps who were shown the door of The Bandolier because of the presence of you, 'a religious gentleman in the corner'. I wonder if their ale-clouded minds allowed them to process a response to being thrown out as they staggered down the road, their evening cut short because a 'holy man' was around? Sadly, we Christians have been rather good at giving the impression that we are heavenly minded party-poopers who believe that fun before death (even good clean fun) is off-limits. Not that a couple of elderly blokes knocking seven bells out of each other would be good, of course, but there are still some followers of Jesus who seem to view any kind of fun with the pursed-lipped disdain that one reserves for a rash that requires cream. People don't tend to associate Christians with anything that's loud, high-spirited or risky. We're expected to be thoroughly 'balanced' and 'conservative' – but I fear that these might be code words for 'bland'. Recently a rather dour gentleman approached me after a sermon where I had used humour (I'm sure this has happened to you, Adrian?) He insisted that we Christians are not to have fun, but joy. He seemed to have neither, and besides, 'deep joy' seems like an unwelcome, prissy second cousin to a full-on belly laugh. And I've met a few Christians who claim to be joyful but whose po-faced expressions suggest that they are trying to pass something the size of a camel. You've been quite the pioneer in getting Christians to laugh. Why do we find it so difficult to relax?

But it's the reaction of Tom, the landlord, which really interests me. As you say, he would have thrown the wrinkly wannabee gladiators out of the snug anyway, because he runs a tight ship, or, in this case, a safe pub for all. But he obviously thought that he was doing you a kindness. He didn't want you to be offended by the cussing codgers, what with you hosting a television show that talked about God. So he jumped in to protect you, not wanting you to be offended by the bad language.

It seems to me that people who are *not* Christians sometimes view those who are with one of two extreme viewpoints – either that we are too weak to cope with the real world or too strong to relate to it.

Let me explain. Some of us give the impression that our faith is so fragile, that we can't possibly be exposed to the rough and tumble of the real world. Experts at haughty looks and tut-tutting, we act like ailing patients. At the other extreme, some Christians give the impression that we are such strong, together human beings. We are people who have arrived rather than those who are still travelling, so we don't swear, lust, get angry or depressed, and act like Dot Cotton at a pole dancing convention when we bump into the great unwashed who do. Perhaps we just need to give each other permission to be the human, messy, in-the-process lovers of God that we are. It might just save some elderly warriors from hypothermia.

While I'm on this, Adrian, I'd like to tell you a recent pub story of my own. Unfortunately it's one of the few stories that I have that makes me look quite good, so please forgive me for that. Most of my anecdotes feature me as a sort of Mr. Bean with a Bible, an entirely inept bloke floating from one epic embarrassment to another. I've written about it elsewhere, so will just give the bare essentials.

I was with Kay (she sends her love) at a national ministers conference in San Diego. There were two thousands pastors and I was one of the speakers. We went to the hotel bar late one night, and three slightly drunk men joined us. First they chatted, telling us all about themselves in the best of spirits. Then they asked Kay why such a beautiful lady had decided to marry someone as old as me. Finally, they swayed over to the karaoke machine and, in full view of the other pastors, one of them dedicated the song they were about to sing to us.

Initially, I was extremely embarrassed. What would the other pastors think? But then I decided that didn't matter. What mattered was that these three wanted to spend time with us. It taught me a lesson . . .

Like you, I'd like to be someone that people who don't know God want to be around. That doesn't mean that our lives should never present a challenge to them; we're called to be the salt of the earth, not sugar. I'm not suggesting that we adopt a bland compliance where we look and sound just exactly like everyone else, just because we want to fit in.

But the song dedication and the chat shared that night nudges me to pray that God will make me someone who is winsome enough to be worthy of some unexpected party and dinner invitations, which of course is what happened to the Jesus we follow. But that will always be a little dangerous. Hanging out with the unholy meant that he was constantly misunderstood by the religious. Yet he wouldn't back off, and was determined to hang out with the 'wrong' crowd, who loved him, and not just because of his legendary capacity for providing great wine at parties. To borrow your analogy of religious people in the corner, Jesus switched corners. Those who follow him are supposed to be like him. And being like him means taking the same risks.

All this talk of religion in corners brings me on to your friend Ted. I was both sad and glad to hear about him losing his faith, and the chat that you shared together. Over the years, I've lost quite a lot of *my* faith. Adrian, you knew me in my early years as a Christian zealot. I could dispense 'answers' like the Milky Bar Kid handing out white chocolate. The contours of my faith were very clear and bold. And I viewed people with the same black and white thinking with which I pondered faith – they were either in or out, good or bad, 'sound' or questionable. The prospect of me confessing to uncertainty or doubt was about as likely as the current Archbishop of Canterbury being used as model for the 'Hairdresser of the Year' competition. I was also very worried about Jesus coming back, Adrian, which made trips to Tesco very scary. Kay would wander off and, after frantically searching for her for ten minutes, I'd be convinced that Jesus had returned. Rats.

Now I'd been left behind, and I was about to be boiled alive in fat for being a Christian. Then I'd find that she had not done a vertical take off, but had been ferreting around in the frozen cabinet in search of fish fingers. My faith back then was a strange cocktail of blind certainty heavily laced with terror (a rather odd combination).

Things have changed. I still remain as convinced about Jesus as ever, (most of the time – I still have my moments when I really hope we're not deluding ourselves) but I do experience a frequent tightening of the buttocks when Christians come up with easy answers to tough questions. Because of this, Kay has banned me from watching certain evangelists who appear on Christian television, mainly because she doesn't like the sight of breakfast cereal dripping down the front of the television.

I was watching one of them recently while eating my Special K with raspberries and skimmed milk (a lot of information, I know, Adrian, but I feel a surge of piety even as I describe such a healthy meal). 'God has shown me a way to avoid trouble and pressure in this world' he ranted, waving a Bible at the camera. The irony of his Bible-waving was not lost on me: it tells the stories of hordes of faithful and faith-filled followers of God who were hunted down, thrown into furnaces, stoned and beaten and even crucified, all of which seems to be both troublesome and pressurised.

Apparently they didn't know the evangelist's secret key to an easy life, which involves phoning a toll-free number and making a dent into a credit card. 'God has put something in your hand that he wants you to send to me', he yelled. I looked at the mushy cereal in my hand. 'No, darling', said Kay, behind me, just in time . . .

Adrian, that kind of stuff makes me want to lose my faith – completely. But even losing *some* of the faith that used to be mine is a scary journey, as I try to let go of the dross and hang on to the gold. In some ways, the old, solid landscape was more comforting. I wonder where my meandering is going to take me.

And then all of this can make life difficult on 'Planet Christian' – you know, being around other believers. I winced three times only yesterday as I chatted with a number of Christians who told me that (a) global warming is a myth, (b) God's going to judge America because he doesn't like Obama, and (c) God has been good to them today. I won't dignify the first two ideas with a comment – but even the third one bewilders me. If God is so good today, does this mean that tomorrow he might have an off-day, and Thursday might be a time of divine naughtiness?

And prayer has become a complete mystery to me – and I don't mean that there are areas of confusion about it; I mean the whole subject has disappeared into a bank of thick fog. My problem used to be with unanswered prayer – but now I'm more bewildered by *answered* prayer. Looking out at a world that screams with hunger and suffering, it stuns me that we in the affluent West get answers about anything at all, never mind reserved parking spaces. And yet . . . we do. God is interested in our trivial pursuits, though God knows why. The hairs on heads are numbered (there's probably an angel with a calculator on my shoulder because of the rapidly reducing number of them. You have a hairstyle. I have a shrinking peninsula).

What obviously *was* a real gift from God, and perhaps an answer to someone's prayer, was your chat with Ted. He had somebody that he could explore with, even doubt with. Most of all, he had someone who was interested in listening to him. I'm sure your little conversational grunts

were very profound grunts, but it sounds like you listened more than you talked.

Sorry, I'm back at the snug again, and those drunk
blokes being hoofed out. Perhaps we need churches
where there is a snug. Where we can have a risky conversation without rushing to make a declaration. Where we
can listen and not just talk at each other. Where we can
rattle on and not feel that we are about to be burned at the
stake as heretics. Where our security comes, not from
holding onto slogans that don't work, but from our sense
that truth can cope with being prodded.

And when I say listen, I mean *really* listen, and not just
go with the flow of what's happening in our world.
Someone wiser than me has said that if you listen to the
conversations between some nations and couples, what
you hear are the dialogues of the deaf. What do you
think?

Thanks for listening to Ted. And to me.

With love,

Jeff

THREE

Dear Jeff,

Your letter was a joy. I devoured it as a hungry man devours the first truly satisfying meal he has managed to get his choppers on for a very long time. I am so zingingly glad that you haven't been healed of flippancy. If ever there was a God-given disease, this must be it. I suffer from the same ailment, and it brings me much joy, although I do have to be careful sometimes. Only the other day Bridget and I were, by some strange oversight, staying in a Christian Bed and Breakfast establishment. When we came down for our bacon and eggs in the morning we were greeted with a large sheet of paper blu-tacked to the dining-room wall, on which was written:

JESUS
HAS
RISEN!

I nearly did it, Jeff. If Bridget hadn't been there (judging by your 'mushy cereal' story, Kay has the same function in your life as Bridget has in mine) and if I had happened to have a pen in my hand at that second, I would have added the words:

AND HE'LL
BE DOWN
IN A MINUTE

I too have been approached on occasions by those who, like your 'dour gentleman', are keen to put me right in this area. Most come from those churches where spontaneity is carefully organised. More than twenty years ago, for instance, not long after *The Sacred Diary of Adrian Plass* had been published, a tall, serious, very thin young man steered me prophetically into a corner after a meeting where, I have to confess, the sin of immoderate laughter had been indulged in, and initiated a dialogue that proceeded in the following manner.

Him: (*with holy severity, and as though he had put the tip of his finger into something disgusting for the sake of the gospel*) I have read your book.

Me: Ah, right. Well – right.

Him: (*with a faint air of puzzlement, but no lightening of his features whatsoever*) It's quite funny.

Me: (*miserably*) Oh, good. That's good. That's . . .

Him: (*earnestly*) Only I don't think non-Christians should be allowed to read it.

Me: Oh, really? Why is that?

Him: Because they might think the church really is like that.

Me: Er . . .

Sometimes, of course, as you will know only too well, Jeff, you run into individuals who have lost their grip in a much more dramatic and disturbing way. I was once greeted in the foyer of a conference centre by a fierce little terrier of a man who barked loudly in my face

'I *hate* you!'

A lesson I have learned from working with disturbed kids, and more recently in ministry (the similarities are bizarrely fascinating) is to metaphorically lean back rather than forwards in situations such as this. A variety of judo, I suppose.

'I don't believe we've met,' I said mildly. 'Why do you hate me?'

'Because,' he growled, 'I don't like the way you laugh at the church in your books.'

I nodded, role-playing humility and willingness to learn, as is my wont.

'I see, so which particular books did you have a problem with?'

Completely unabashed, he replied, 'I haven't read any of them. And I don't want to, because I've heard that you laugh at the church in them.'

I rocked on my heels for a moment, then passed quietly on, feeling that this was unlikely to turn into a productive conversation. Immediately after my first talk in the morning, however, the human Rottweiler addressed me in exactly the same aggressively trenchant tones.

'I *love* you now!'

Stepping forward, he threw his frightening, disproportionately long arms around my body (I was under the hideous impression that they wrapped around me twice, but that can't be right, can it?) and gripped me in a vice-like hug. Every encounter for the next three days began with this extravagant gesture. I think I preferred him when he hated me . . .

So, why are we flippant, you and I? I suspect it's because we are not flippant at all about the things that matter. I am boringly serious about following Jesus, and

tediously orthodox in my faith, but I have learned that
laughter can clear away an awful lot of the rubbish that
threatens to overwhelm the central truths that never die.

Where can you find that truth in this beautiful, weari-
some world? I think there's a clue in your story about the
karaoke evening. I love that story, Jeff. So sweet and right
and open-ended and filled with Jesus. It made me think
of times when people have asked me which feature film
has inspired me most as a Christian. When I tell them that
it's *The Commitments*, they look a little puzzled. This film,
as you probably know, is about a group of young people
in Ireland struggling to get a band together and hit the
big-time. Wonderfully funny and always entertaining, the
film is also filled with unrestrained swearing and explicit
sexual references. There are occasional moments of
extreme violence.

Well, whatever there is in it, it makes me cry and it
makes me pray. It makes me realise that Jesus is as determined to be among hopeful, passionate, troubled human
beings like that in this age, as he was when he walked the
earth as a man two thousand years ago. I have comment-
ed elsewhere on Lionel Blue's statement that Judaism is
not his prison, it is his home. When you feel safe at home
you can go to any other place on earth and never forget
where you really belong, nor be separated from the love
that will protect the most important part of you wherever you are and whatever happens to you. Conversely,
where the church has become a garrison, most of our
energy is spent either on making sure that nobody unde-
sirable can get in, or on making lists of rules and constantly, worriedly, tidying up.

You asked in your letter why Christians find it so difficult to relax, Jeff. I wonder if the answer to that question
has something to do with this frantic desire to keep things

tidy and organised. Which reminds me. I was recently challenged on two things that Bridget and I had said or suggested in the course of a church weekend. The first of these was about Elijah, a bit of a favourite of yours I seem to remember.

Elijah is usually described as one of the 'great' prophets, but we wanted to explore what that might mean. I recently wrote Bible notes on the specific subject of Elijah, and became fascinated by the chasm of inadequacy between his heroic spiritual achievements and a general tendency to run away or give up when danger threatened. After dramatically defeating the prophets of Baal on Mount Carmel, for instance, he ran like a chicken from the wrath of Jezebel and ended up sitting under a tree, saying that he had 'had enough'. What, one might reasonably ask, was the matter with the man? This was the God who had supplied food from a flying larder, prov-ided a miraculously bottomless container of oil, healed a dead son, caused rain in the midst of a drought and rained divine fire onto the mountain. Why on earth should he be incapable of dealing with one cross little queen?

The answer appears to be something about the presence or absence of the Spirit of God. When a job needed to be done and Elijah was filled with the Spirit, anything was possible. In the gaps between these supernaturally direc-ted and infused events, he became exactly what he was, a not very adequate, less than courageous human being. As a less than adequate and sometimes very fearful human being myself, I found this realisation helpful. The good news, we suggested to people at the weekend away, is that God can use us whatever our weaknesses and fears, as long as we are willing to be obedient when the time comes for action. Good news for most of us useless specimens, don't you think? Scary, no doubt, but ultimately good.

My challenger wanted to know if I didn't agree that Elijah's fear and self-doubt were actually lies from the evil one, designed to distract him from the tasks in hand. I got the distinct impression that she not only wanted, but *needed* to stick this label on the inconveniently negative and unruly nature of Elijah's faults and weaknesses.

So, did I agree with her? Should I have done? Granted, there is a bit in the Gospel of John about Satan being the father of lies, but does that mean I ought to deny and refuse to believe in the bundle of faults and proclivities and patterns and tendencies that, for one reason or another, make up the person that I am? Is there some spiritual conjuring trick whereby I can tell myself that because I am a new creature in Christ the old me simply doesn't exist? Try it, Jeff. See how you get on.

I read somewhere once that God loves us exactly as we are, and far too much to leave us as we are. Well, I certainly go along with that, but the process of change is a gradual one, and if it isn't spiritually *and* humanly organic, it has nothing to do with a God who loves us for who we are, as well as in spite of our deficiencies. In the meantime, I reckon you and I and everyone else can be cheered and encouraged by the message of Elijah, that there will be times when, if we are obedient, the Spirit of God will fill us and even work miracles through us, regardless of the fact that we fall so far short of the ideal.

So, no, I didn't agree.

The second challenge, or question, was connected with things we had said about the grace of God. We offered an explanatory picture. For those engaged on the journey of life there are three options. On one side are the impassable rocks and mountains of the law. No good taking that route. It's too difficult and you won't make it. On the other side is the swamp of licence. It looks okay on the surface, but try going that way and you'll sink and suffocate and die. Right down the middle runs the narrow path of grace, a way that springs from the undeserved kindness of God, and is individually designed for each person who needs it. An example we put forward was Jesus' handling of the situation where an adulterous woman was condemned to stoning. He didn't dispute the law or condone what she'd done, but he did find a typically ingenious and authentic way to rescue her from the consequences of sin. Grace, we suggested, is creative, relational, constructive, surprising and redemptive, and each of us is responsible for offering it to the people we encounter.

My challenger wanted to know if I felt this applied to homosexuals as well. Surely there could be no compromise over an issue that is so clearly condemned in Scripture. Not, she added, that she would personally condemn such people. There was a gay couple in her church, and they were perfectly nice people. On the other hand, unrepented sin was unrepented sin, and she would not feel it right for them to be publicly representing the church, by sitting on the Parochial Church Council, for instance.

Here we go again, I thought. Why do issues of sex in general and sexuality in particular continually dominate the moral agenda in some sections of the church? In Corinthians Paul says that we mustn't associate with a brother who is sexually immoral or greedy, an idolater or a slanderer, a drunkard or a swindler. How many candidates for membership of the Parochial Church Council are carefully vetted for any evidence of greed, gossip, excessive drinking or devious practices in business? How many replacements would have to be found if they were? The mind boggles.

I know a lot of gay Christians who have made a decision to remain celibate for the rest of their lives. Satan may or may not be telling them lies about their sexual preferences, but the fact is that, however hard they pray and do their best to embrace change, they appear to be stuck with being who and what they are, and every day is a challenge and a battle. I have a great respect for them. I also know gay Christians who believe that same-sex relationships are acceptable to God. I have a great respect for anyone who makes a genuinely thoughtful and prayerful decision about any aspect of their Christian lives, even when I don't actually agree with them. My own decisions have been rubbish sometimes, and I've usually defended them loudly from the Bible.

What about the grace of God? Well, the trouble with God is, and always has been, that he will stubbornly insist on dealing with people as individuals instead of categories. Grace will do what grace will do. I find that warming and exciting and reassuring and disturbing and a bit confusing, but I honestly wouldn't want it any other way.

If I ever meet my challenger again, I shall thank her for making me think about these things, but I would also like to remind her that over the last two thousand years, many people have tried to clean and tidy the Christian faith as one might clean and tidy a house. Sorry, I would say, it can't be done. If Christ in chaos is not a genuine option we are in a lot of trouble.

You're right, Jeff. Every church should have a 'snug', a place where you can risk saying and thinking and feeling whatever is on your heart. That may take a while to set up, but in the meantime we seem to be creating one of our own. This is a very comfortable corner. Your round, I think.

Love,

Adrian

PS: I did feel for you when the karaoke fellows wondered why someone like Kay was hanging around with an old bloke like you. During a tour in Germany a couple of years ago they used a very old photograph of me for the publicity. The first question from the floor at the beginning of the second half of the evening went as follows: 'Why did you send your father instead of coming yourself?'

He got the biggest laugh of the evening.

FOUR

Dear Adrian,

Thanks for yours, which inspired me to pop down to my local video store (so-called despite them not being purveyors of videos any more, since the advent of the mighty DVD) to rent a copy of *The Commitments*. While in the store something happened that has absolutely nothing whatsoever to do with anything important, but it amused me, so allow me to tell you about it. Believe me, what follows is the truth.

Clutching my DVD (they didn't have *The Commitments*), I lined up to part with some cash, and it was then that I noticed a sticker on the DVD case. 'Be kind, rewind', it said. The sight of it confused me deeply, because it is quite impossible to rewind a DVD. So why the rewind sticker? I decided to enquire of the nine-year-old who was serving behind the counter.

The following conversation took place with that somewhat uninterested acne-fighting youth:

Me: Excuse me, could I ask you about this sticker?
Spotty youth: Yeah, what about it?
Me: Well, it says, 'Be kind, rewind.'
Spotty youth: Right. It does.

Me: But that's silly.

Spotty youth: What? Why?

Me: Because this is a DVD, it is therefore impossible for
      one to rewind it.

Spotty youth: (*rolling his eyes*) Of course you can't rewind
      a DVD. It's a DVD.

Me: Er, yes, that's what I just said. So why put the sticker
      on the DVD case, which is likely to confuse people,
      and prompt them to ask questions about it?

Spotty youth: It's simple. When we stopped doing videos
      and changed over to DVDs, we had hundreds of
      these stickers left over, and the boss didn't want to
      waste them, seeing as we'd paid to have them
      printed, so she made us put the stickers on the
      DVDs . . .

Me: So your boss paid for stickers that are now redun-
      dant and then paid yet more money in staff time to
      place these useless stickers on DVD cases that are
      likely to confuse customers like me?

Spotty youth: (*looking over my shoulder at the customer
      behind me with a look that says 'I've got a right one
      here'*) You got it. We used up the leftover stickers.
      Any other questions?

Like I said Adrian, this interchange has no relevance to
our ongoing chat whatsoever, but it was so utterly bizarre
that I just had to share it with you.

Thinking about you in that Bed and Breakfast, how I
wish you had summoned up the courage to add a bit of
cheeky graffiti to the 'He has risen' sign, although I suppose this might have been taking our mutually shared
gift of flippancy a step too far. At least, as sayings go,
'He has risen' isn't cheesy, and it is the truth. In my early
days as a Christian, I used to sport a large badge almost

the size of a dustbin lid. It screamed a very unsubtle message – something like 'Hello, you're going to hell'. I was quite into badges and paraphernalia acquired from the local Christian bookshop. I had so many fishes on the back of my car, it looked like a mobile aquarium. (By the way, my local bookstore is currently selling breath mints with Scriptures printed on them. They're called 'Testamints' and the package says they are 'changing the world one mint at a time' . . . If only these had been available when Paul was around. He could have been even more effective in church planting and avoided halitosis too . . .)

I digress. Back to signs and slogans. I'm a keen observer of church signboards, especially in America, and I've seen some corkers in my time. During a heat wave in Oklahoma, during which some people died, one congregation who were determined to be 'good news' had this sign up outside their building

If You Think It Is Hot Here, Just Wait

This is almost as bad as the pithy but brutal sign that screamed

Eternity: Smoking or Non-Smoking?

that I spotted outside another church building.

This Christian habit of graphic ranting has spawned a few amusing take-offs, though. My personal favourites are the bumper stickers that announce

Jesus Is Coming, Look Busy

Or even

Jesus Loves You. The Rest Of Us Think You Are An
&%$@&

More seriously, I was so sorry to hear about your encounter with the little man you describe as a 'terrier'. It's a perfect description, because there are some religious people who delight in nipping at your ankles, get excited over little tidbits and, once they've got their teeth into you, refuse to let go. I expect that between us we've bumped into enough terriers to fill Battersea Dogs' Home. Perhaps you've got thicker skin than me, (although I somehow doubt that), but those nips and bites hurt. Your story about the terrier who said that he *hated* you (and then, unfortunately, decided to love you) took my breath away.

I've been nibbled around the ankles a few times myself over the years, and sometimes people get very personal. You mentioned the chap who made the comment about you looking old enough to be your father. One lady came up to me after I'd preached and asked me if I'd ever suffered a stroke. I replied that I had not, and asked her why she'd asked. She replied, 'When you smile, Jeff, only one side of your face goes up.' I desperately wanted to inform her that I was naturally ugly, and ask what her excuse was, but we can't do that, can we? We have to be Christian. How would it be if we asked God if we could have half an hour off every week, and a month of carnality in leap years? No, it's a bad idea . . .

But that was just a little nip compared to the nasty bite I got after preaching in one church, and the irony is that I never spotted the Alsatian who took a chunk out of me. He (or she) just snapped at me and fled before I could even say, 'Down boy!' The mad dog concerned didn't even have the courage to approach me personally, but left an unsigned note (I can't stand anonymous letters, they are so cowardly) on the book table. It was neatly folded, with razor sharp creases that hinted at the acerbic contents within. It simply said

> Sir, We would see Jesus, and not your nonsensical gibberish. You can't win souls to Jesus with all that foolishness. You are not a preacher, you are a comedian. You have missed your calling.

It's pathetic to admit it, but that little dart from the dark reduced me to tears. But no doubt the person who wrote it thought that they had been faithful to the truth, at least as they saw it. And that brings me back to this idea of sharing 'truth'. We've been chatting about the churches needing to have 'snugs', places where you can say whatever is on your mind, without fear of reprisal. But isn't there a need for a note of caution here, because some Christians go around 'telling the truth' and do great damage. These days when someone tells me that they are about to 'speak the truth in love', I look for the nearest nuclear fallout shelter. Their preface about 'speaking in love' usually means that they won't.

Have you ever been in one of those Christian gatherings where the preacher talks about forgiveness and reconciliation, and then the service ends with an excruciating time when everyone is encouraged to 'Go to someone who has offended you' in order to kiss and make up? These buttock-clenching occasions give clumsy (or vindictive) people an ideal opportunity to say 'By the way, I've hated you for years. Please forgive me.' They can vent their spleen (whatever that means) and feel pious about it at the same time. If someone marches up to me and 'confesses' that they've hated me, how does that help me? I'd be better off continuing in ignorance. They walk away, pleased to have got their stuff off their chest, and I'm left reeling. And sometimes these moments go horribly wrong, even before a word has been spoken . . .

At one large Christian event (which shall be nameless but happens in the springtime when they bring the harvest in), one platform personality, who had a reputation for being notoriously difficult, had so many people naffed off with them (and wanting to confess it) that a long queue formed. Imagine that – being so omnidirectionally unpopular that people had to take a number, like at the cheese counter in Tescos, and get in line to tell you how much they hate you. How easily we corrupt even beautiful things, like peace and reconciliation.

And that's why I breathe such a sigh of relief when you talk about God meeting us in our mess. Holiness and mess co-exist. Recently I discovered these words from Archbishop Rowan Williams (he of strange haircut fame, who appears to have a brain the size of a planet)

A human being is holy not because he or she triumphs by will power over chaos and guilt and leads a flawless life, but because that life shows the victory of God's faithfulness *in the midst* of disorder and imperfection. The church is holy . . . .not because it is the gathering of the good and the well behaved, but because it speaks of the triumph of grace in the coming together of strangers and sinners, who miraculously trust one another enough to join in common repentance and common praise . . . Humanly speaking, holiness is always like this: God's endurance in the middle of our refusal of him, his capacity to meet every refusal with the gift of himself.[1]

Forgive the long quote, but I include it because (a) I think it's beautifully put and (b) I wish I had ten per cent of his eminences' brains (see, for me, even moments of insight can be tainted with ambition and envy).

Sometimes I think we Christians only like to think about our being messy in the past tense, like we *were* messy, but then Jesus showed up and we're nice now. Grace didn't just save us, but is ours second-by-second, with all of our ongoing mess and rubbish.

I try to be open about my messiness these days and, generally speaking, I hear a sigh of relief when I share my struggles. I'm both glad (and worried) by the fact that some people are kind enough to tell me that I'm a breath of fresh air, and that they appreciate the authenticity that I try to bring. But that makes me really anxious about the state of the church, because I worry what those who find reality unusual and refreshing are being drip-fed daily. I confess that I've struggled with being vulnerable at times (it's always costly, isn't it?) because I try to take seriously all that the Bible says about Christian leaders setting an example; but surely being an *example* is not the same as projecting a false *image*. And I want to be redemptive in my messiness, if that makes sense. If I stand up and say 'I'm rubbish, and I intend to stay that way and sin to an Olympic level. Who wants to come along for the ride?', then I'm betraying the very heart of the message of Jesus. He lovingly wants to shape and, yes, *change* me. But if I just give off an impression that I am better than I am, then surely all I do is dishearten everyone who listens to me. At least I think that's the way it works. But then I don't want to be guilty of simply washing my dirty laundry in public . . .

Picking up on the comment from the man who said he hated you, this is not just because you've helped the church to see her foibles and follies, but because you are honest about yourself and your own struggles and fears.

Perhaps your willingness to be fragile makes some feel uncomfortable about their own hidden flaws. Or maybe they think that your in-the-process confessions somehow 'let down' the gospel, because some Christians think that we're all supposed to be fixed, shiny, 'tropies of grace'. How do you handle the call not only to flippancy but to transparency?

I totally agree that we want everything to be neat and tidy, and would like to manage grace and direct it to those who deserve it – which is, of course, a contradiction in terms. And when we do that, we end up with lots of ridiculous little rules and regulations – what *Zen and the Art of Motorcycle Maintenance* calls 'itsy-bitsy rules for itsy-bitsy people'. Jesus was hemmed in by the people who were experts at making religion into an exhausting fuss – the Pharisees. They had rules about how much one could greet a bride on her wedding day, and how to comfort a widow at a funeral. They pondered such weighty questions as whether one could pray while working in the top of a tree? Could a man divorce his wife for burning a meal? And (get this one), if someone makes bread while naked, and then wants to use that bread for an offering, is it unclean? That one's been worrying me for a while . . . Surely all of this was done to try to control the mess, and determine what 'good' people look like. Tick this box, and hooray, you're holy, and therefore part of the in-crowd. But, like all systems, it was doomed to failure because, as you say, grace does its work uniquely in each individual. God writes one-off poems, he doesn't create systems.

Perhaps my 'Be kind, rewind' story does have some relevance after all. Just as applying those defunct labels was useless, time-wasting and confusing, so religion can be that. Then we end up puffing and panting our way through life, pursuing the irrelevant and unimportant. Perhaps that's why our gift of flippancy has some merit; as we laugh, primarily at ourselves, we dig away at the crusty irrelevance and pomposity that religion can create, and we go in search of what's at the heart of it all. We mine for what matters.

How wonderful to know that God uses all of us in our messiness – not as the exception, but as the rule. Hence the Bible tells the stories not of a series of beaming, air-brushed heroes, but flawed, confused, geniuses/idiots who got it right and then got it wrong in the next second. As you say, one of the best examples of that is Elijah.

Right, Adrian, enough for now. One of these days I'd love to reflect a little more on the titanic collapse of Elijah – and I love that phrase you use: 'Grace . . . is creative, relational, constructive, surprising and redemptive, and each of us is responsible for offering it to the people we encounter.' That one kept me awake last night . . .

Much love to you,
Jeff

FIVE

Dear Adrian,

Okay, I know it's not my round. But your wonderful description of 'creative grace' has stirred the memory of one of the most poignant moments of my life, when someone went out of their way to creatively demonstrate loving kindness – which is the root of grace – in my life.

That someone was my father. He was stunned and angry when I became a Christian as a teenager. Looking back, I don't blame him. He probably thought that I'd signed my soul over to a weird cult, and saw my conversion as a betrayal of my upbringing. I'm sad to admit that he quickly became my evangelistic project. So desperate was I to introduce him to the heavenly news, I gave him hell. He patiently sat through my urgent monologues, smiled kindly, and told me that he was worried that I was throwing away my life on a myth. He'd not had an easy time in life himself, and he was desperate that I not waste mine. Captured in the African desert at the age of nineteen, he sat and watched his youth rot away in Italian and German prisoner of war camps until, forced to take desperate measures to avoid execution, he escaped, worked his way across Germany, and got home just before the war ended. I've wondered about those four years when he lived close to starvation; he never talked much about those terrible days. Occasionally, when pushed, he'd describe an incident that happened, but he never did tell me about how he *felt*. Sometimes I wonder why, Adrian. Did he shut down some emotions to avoid revisiting all that horror and uncertainty? Or have later generations become more verbal, and perhaps a little too obsessed with process and therapy?

Anyway, he did tell me that he could never believe in God after the terrible things that he'd seen in the war. Twenty years after my brash evangelistic efforts began (and not as a result of them but probably despite them), my dad finally became a Christian – that's another story. Suffice it to say it was a happy, happy day. Now this somewhat Victorian man softened, and he became very open and expressive about his love for me. And then he was hit by a massive stroke. He had always loved to talk and had an opinion about everything. Now he was reduced to spouting endless gibberish. I can remember long telephone conversations where he would jabber on and I would nod and grunt and agree, and he and I would both cry – tears were the only common language we had left – because we knew that we couldn't communicate, and probably never would again. The doctors said he'd probably never recover his speech. They guessed right. The young man who had spent four years behind barbed wire was now in yet another prison; he was to die in that cold cell, trapped and mute until the end.

But not quite. He planned one more big escape.

One night I was staying at my parents' home. It was late, and I was just drifting off to sleep – and there was a knock on my bedroom door. It was my dad. As I asked him to come in, I wondered what he could possibly want – after all, a chat to end the day was impossible.

Figuratively speaking, my dad had found a gap in the electric fence, a way to creatively communicate love and grace to me. He came in, knelt down beside my bed, his face wreathed in a huge smile. And then, Adrian, he tucked me in.

There I was, a forty-year old man with children of my own and a mortgage, and he took the blankets and the sheets, and tucked me in. Then he leaned over, banished a stray hair on my brow, and kissed me once on the cheek. Then, with another broad smile, he was gone. It was quite marvellous.

I was able to return the favour. Some months later, I entered his room without knocking, because he was semi-conscious. They'd turned the lights down in that hospital room so that he wouldn't have to die in the florescent glare. Knowing that he had just hours to live, I decided to do one last thing for him. I tucked *him* in. I took the blankets and the sheet, kissed him lightly on the cheek, and whispered in his ear: 'Go now, Dad. Get out of here. No more pain for you. You don't need to fight. Jesus makes you safe.'

And within minutes he went.

I'm sharing this, Adrian, because I think that we can all find ways to share grace creatively. It's not just for the strong, or the clever, to pass kindness around. And when we find ways to do that, others are changed by our efforts. I still feel the warmth of that single kiss to this day.

With much love,
Jeff

SIX

Dear Jeff,

Forgive me. Bridget and I were away working just after your last letter but one arrived, and then the next one turned up before I had a chance to reply. I'm glad it happened like that actually, because those two letters confirmed and revealed an aspect of your personality that some people might find quite surprising. The besieged individual who wrote that venom-filled anonymous note after your talk (perhaps we should combine the words 'venom' and 'anonymous' to form the new adjective 'venomynous') might well have been amazed to discover how those thirty-four simple words reduced you to tears. We bigheaded gits who stand up in front of loads of people and bleat on and on about God are popularly supposed to be very confident types. I suppose we must be in a way, or we wouldn't be able to go on doing it. However, there is a fragility in the structure of this apparent confidence that is, I suspect, induced by a particular tension that Christian speakers have to deal with constantly if they truly care about what they are doing.

And it is this: we can never match our message. That is the temporal but, thank God, not eternal problem for people like you and I. Poor old Elijah as well, of course, on a slightly larger scale. It certainly is for me. I have a head like a barrage balloon and the heart of a puzzled child. I can so easily be hurt and, as your two letters illustrate with crystal clarity, Jeff, so can you. After reading that wonderful passage from Rowan Williams (he's such a *good* man, isn't he?) I hesitate to inflict a quote from one of my own books on you, but it does sum up what I'm trying to say. It's from a Bible note about Peter's denials in the courtyard, and it finishes with the following words

> I know now that the only thing I can offer God is myself, and he will gladly, smilingly welcome that self, but the child in me wanted so much to be *good enough*. I find it painfully difficult to accept that God called me in the full knowledge that I was bound to let him down and betray him at one time or another. How hard it is for people as proud as many of us are to be *known* to such a depth – to feel all our human defences, tricks and pretences being gradually stripped away, and to see the naked poverty that is our real condition. We mourn for our spurious human dignity even as we plead for it to be removed.
>
> Separated by two thousand years and nothing at all, Peter and I, and many others, go out and weep bitterly together because we fail our Master and because he always knew that we would.[2]

In the same letter you described the hideous business of trying to bully people into forgiveness. We know one or two people who have been terribly hurt by this kind of nonsense. Just recently, after speaking at a church in the north, I was approached by a lady who sat next to me and, after checking that no one in authority was listening, spoke from behind her hand in worriedly hushed tones.

'Adrian,' she whispered, 'I only became a Christian a couple of months ago, and they've told me I've got to forgive everybody. Everybody! The thing is – I can't. Not just like that. I've been so hurt in the past. I can't just pretend to feel all right about it, can I? The thing that worries me, though, is they say Jesus said I can't be forgiven if I don't forgive others, so what can I do?'

Not for the first time I imagined the benefit of installing loudspeakers over some church porches from which a recorded voice, rather in the style of that familiar London Underground announcement, would issue the warning, 'Mind the crap!'

The thing is, I explained to my troubled new friend, those who had told her this were technically absolutely right. Jesus does say that we must forgive our enemies, and he does indeed make it clear that God will not forgive us if we don't. What they had clearly failed to point out was that God does not apply penalties and punishments in the heartless style that we have come to expect from bank and building society computers. In fact, in one sense, God is more like the old-fashioned bank managers who were prepared to offer customers all sorts of help and support *as long as they stayed in touch.*

'Go to God,' I suggested, 'and say something like this – be completely honest. "God, it says in the Bible that I should forgive my enemies. If that's what you really want me to do, then that's what I want as well, but at the moment I can't. There are people in my past who hurt me so much that I'd like them to die, and I'd like to be there to watch. Jesus says we must love our enemies and pray for them. For now, I don't really know what loving them means, but I'm going to do what you say. I'm going to grit my teeth and ask you to give them the best of everything they need, even though I don't mean it and I hate them as much as I ever did. I know it's only one rung of the ladder, Father, but it's all I can manage for now. Help me to climb a bit further every day. Thank you. Amen."'

God is so much nicer and more accommodating than his followers, don't you think, Jeff? He must be almost as nice as my mother was – possibly even a little nicer, although I don't want to get carried away.

As to this most recent letter, Jeff, what can I say? A couple of miserable blubbers, you and I are. Your beautifully written account of those two significant encounters with your dad reduced me to tears and excavated my emotional entrails (sorry about the disgusting metaphor) in all sorts of ways. I wish I was able to write about my father with the same passion and warmth. I can't. In fact, I find it almost impossible to discuss or write anything about that aspect of my life, and I'm not going to try at the moment. It's not about forgiveness. I wish it was. One day, perhaps, when you and I are sitting in a real snug under the regal Harvey's banner, I might have a go. We'll see. Sorry to be so feeble but there it is. You only have to touch some scars and they turn into open wounds.

On another level, that chunk of your history did send me journeying into my own past in pursuance of a personal mission that began many years ago and will probably not end on this side of the grave. I guess it's something to do with the business of setting aside one's personal agenda. Pious and impossibly ambitious as it might seem, I really do want to have and to submit to the mind of Christ, and I don't want my silly little templates of behaviour or attitude to get in the way.

I have an example of the kind of thing I mean.

You come to realise that some memories are indeed like templates. They are formed from experiences so pungently significant that they have engraved a pattern of success or failure or survival into the very stuff of what you are. Sound silly, Jeff? Maybe it is a bit over the top, but consider this. I postponed facing up to the story I am about to tell you for years. Why? Because I was frightened. I was frightened of discovering that the things I do and the person I am were shaped and signposted more than fifty years ago, by circumstances and pressures that have little or nothing to do with the Christian faith that is supposed to have directed and informed my life. This is what happened.

I was about nine years old. It was a Saturday afternoon in Rusthall, the village where I grew up. I'd been playing with my friends Paul and David among the bracken up on the common. Remember bracken? It was great. You could make excellent spears with it, if you ripped off all but the fronds at the thin end of the plant, and then there was the delicious cosiness of creating bracken nests, where you could squat silently and invisibly, as people passed along the nearby path that ran from Langton Road down into the village . . .

After playing on the common we headed, hot and scruffy, to Paul's house for a drink. His parents were better off than ours, so we might enjoy the unusual luxury of a choice of drinks when we got to his home. Lemonade *or* orange squash. That would be good.

We were disappointed. Paul's mum and dad were out, and he had no key. Paul found a piece of wood and a manky old ball in his back garden. We decided to have a game of French cricket on the concrete driveway, running down the side of the house, from the garage to the High Street. His mum would probably be back soon and then we'd get that drink.

Our game was interrupted by the appearance of a boy called Richard Adams, who must have seen us playing as he passed sullenly by on the High Street. We didn't like Richard much. He was bigger and rougher than us and, although we could never have expressed it at the time, there was an aura of bitterness and resentment in him that made us uncomfortable. Someone, his truculent manner suggested, was going to have to pay for whatever had so disastrously happened or not happened in his life.

Richard had collected a handful of small stones which he began to shy at us with malicious, wordless intensity and alarming accuracy. The stones were sharp and they hurt. None of us were fighting types, Paul least of all. After receiving two or three of these stinging missiles on soft parts of his body, he opened the unlocked garage door and ducked inside, calling in a strangled voice for us to join him. David hastily followed. I didn't. I closed the garage door from the outside and, turning, stood with my back to it, an easy target for Richard, who had temporarily run out of ammunition and was busy rearming himself from the gulley at the side of the driveway.

I avoided some of the stones that were thrown after that, but quite a lot of them hit me in the face, body and legs. It was agony. I just stood there until my aggressor got bored and wandered away, mumbling darkly to himself. Paul and David came out as soon as Paul's mum came back.

So there it is. That's what happened. Pretty insignificant on the face of it, Jeff. Why does it trouble me so much? Why has the memory of that incident nagged at me for years? I think it has something to do with my motivation for enduring all that pain when I could have hidden safely in the garage with the others. Leaving aside the fact that I had definitely read far too much Victorian and Edwardian literature about heroic schoolboys, I probably felt I had discovered a new way to solve problems for other people.

It's easy. You simply remove them – the people, that is.
You tuck them safely away from the firing line and then
face all the flak yourself until the problem eases or goes
away. After all, what does it matter if it hurts you for a
while? Pain passes. The important thing is that you've
solved the problem for the others, or at least made it dis-
appear for a time. It has absolutely nothing to do with
bravery because, looking back, I see this same pattern or
template in the work I did with children in care, in the
parenting of my own children, and in the writing and
speaking that I have done over the last twenty years.
What if I publicly endure the painful shrapnel of confusion and doubt and fear? What does it really matter, as
long as the others are safely hidden behind the garage
doors? They can come out as soon as the danger passes.
Then we can carry on playing French cricket as though
nothing ever happened. And, as I have already said, it
requires no courage on my part, just a decision that I will
do it in my own rather curiously contradictory and con-
trolling way.

Did God draw the template or did I? Is it right? Does it
work? Does it matter? Does God use it or work round it?
Am I a complete loony? Those are the immediate questions. I suspect that God, being God, will expect me to
push through to find some answers. I have none at present.

One more thought, following on from the letter about
your dad. The other night I was in a Bible study group
where we were discussing that bit after the Sermon on the
Mount where Jesus says that we only have to ask and
God will give us what we need. Human fathers give good
gifts to their offspring, he goes on to say, so how much
more will our heavenly Father give generously to his children?

A member of the group talked about a friend who is dying of cancer, and wondered why a God who promises so much has failed to answer the heartfelt prayers of all the people who love this sufferer. I am all too familiar with the list of no doubt deeply meaningful answers, some slick and some saggy, that we habitually dole out in response to this question. I've used them myself. So have you, I expect, Jeff. Forgetting that utilitarian catalogue for a moment, I was reminded of all the good and faithful people I've met who are genuinely committed to the notion of God as Father, but are continually baffled and disappointed by his apparent failure to break into what appear to be randomly occurring events in their lives and the lives of others.

Throughout the corporately optimistic world of evangelical Christianity, I detect evidence of heartfelt yearning for a '*Railway Children* moment', that wonderful moment when the mist parts and the air is filled with the richest, best kind of magic, and we cry, 'Daddy, my daddy!' to the one we have thought about and talked about and read about and tried to understand and longed to be close to for such a very long time.

It's the right thing to want, don't you think, whatever they shout from the parapets of embattled Christianity? I trust Jesus more than I trust those spiritual agoraphobics. He makes dreams come true.

Thanks so much for that last letter, Jeff.

God bless you,
Adrian

SEVEN

Dear Adrian,

Thanks for yours. Your words had the effect of one of those lovely Catherine Wheel fireworks that I recall nostalgically from Bonfire Night (I can smell the hot dogs, onions and tomato ketchup even now). Those spinning pinwheels rotate furiously and spit fire and light everywhere. Your letter did that – it scattered a shower of sparks in my head, setting me off on a series of thoughts, some absurd, some perhaps not so. Let's take the ridiculous before the sublime (okay, I may never get anywhere near the sublime).

I'm so sorry to hear about your entrails. I shall add them to my prayer list. The next time I'm in church and someone asks if there are any prayer requests, you'll be glad to know that we shall lift the Plass bowels heavenward. Of course I jest, but the construction of this silly paragraph reminds me of one time when a dear lady, during a well-attended service that I took part in, requested intercessory activity on behalf of her son's twisted testicles. The unfortunate lad was present, and squirmed with embarrassment as the whole church proceeded to storm heaven's gates for the deliverance of his tragically knotted undercarriage. Some of the men in the church even wept as they prayed, with obvious empathy. Perhaps, Adrian, this knotting up of one's nether regions is a common problem. I shall not ask you if you've personally experienced any confusion in the lower parts yourself. I however, have met quite a few Christians who have apparently got their bits in quite a twist. Those 'venomynous' people (love your new word) that we've bumped into over the years may well have had some knots of their own to deal with.

More seriously, I was moved and actually angered to read about your horrible experience of being stoned. Reading about it, even all these years after it happened, made me want to go out and find that nauseous bully, Richard Adams. Perhaps we could trace him through the Internet; put his name in the *Enemies Reunited* site, and then pop round and deliver an evangelistic tract (wrapped in a brick). We could then ask for forgiveness.

It's quite the thought, Adrian, you as a schoolboy hero, a junior Superman without the blue tights, your back against that garage door as the odious Richard rained his missiles down upon you. It was very brave, you taking the pounding and protecting your friends. But then I started to wonder what *they* were thinking and doing while you did your version of Custer's Last Stand. They must have heard the stones slamming into the garage door, and perhaps even heard your cries as yet another missile hit you in the face or body. Why didn't they come out and help you? Why didn't the three of you combine forces and give that bully a bullying? Were your feelings of relief when Adams moved on replaced by irritation and disappointment ('How come you chaps left me stranded?') I say that because, as we've talked about being hurt, I've found it a gazillion times harder to be wounded *by* the church than being wounded *for* the church. When those who are supposed to be fellow family members hurt me or desert me, I bleed more copiously. That prompts a question: how do you hang on to hope for the ragamuffin, wonderful, ridiculous, beautiful bride/hag that is the church? Some Christians throw in the towel when it comes to St. Whatsit's and make the snug of The Dog and Duck their church. Are you ever tempted to join them permanently?

And then I wondered (as you do still) about *why* you just stood there that day. I have to confess that, if I had done that, it would probably have been for mixed motives. My nobility would have been tainted with less heroic ambitions. For one thing, to turn and run might have looked cowardly – so I might have been too worried about what I looked like. I would have wanted not only to be the hero, but to be clearly *seen* to be the hero. You mentioned the Sermon on the Mount. Like the Pharisee who hires the Acker Bilk and his Paramount Jazz band to play a screaming clarinet tune to announce that he's dropping ten pence into the offering, or who dabs his face with Max Factor 'Colour of Death' powder to let the world know that he's fasting, I'd like the delicious reward of being *seen* to be good. It takes real character to be good in secret, doesn't it?

And then, to scamper into the garage would have demanded that I turn my back on the evil Adams. For a few terrible seconds, I would not be able to see where the stones were heading, and so wouldn't be able to try to dodge them. All of this brings me back to your core question: why do we do what we do? Is it for pure motives? I'm certain that I've never done anything for totally right reasons. Even at my highest heights of holiness (whatever they are or look like) there's a sneaky, furtive little mission to look good, to be congratulated, sometimes even to do better than others. I might be painting myself in overly grim colours, but I do know that self is the irritating stain that is so difficult to wash out of me. Actually, sometimes I feel like giving up, not because of the stone-throwing of others, but because I get exhausted with the unfinished business that is my life. And it's made worse when others make it all seem so easy, such a neat process, as if 'spiritual growth' is a brisk march up a straight path that climbs to the top of Everest, a straight line on a graph. I don't march or walk with Jesus; I stagger, and take frequent rest stops. And sometimes I can identify with Charlie Brown in the Peanuts cartoon. Stopping by Lucy's 'five cents for psychological advice' stall, he's told that he needs to know where he is going in life. Lucy advises him that some people navigate life with their deckchair at the front of the ship – they are the ones who can see where they are going. Others, of course, prefer to locate their deckchair at the stern of the ship, so they can ponder where they have been. Charlie is bewildered at this profound advice, and announces that he can't even get the deckchair unfolded. I love Charlie.

Perhaps, while pursuing perfection (to quote Jesus, although that 'Be perfect' comment in the Sermon on the Mount tended to tower over me like a mountain, before I understood it as a visionary call rather than an impossible demand), we also have to make peace with failure, without selling out to it. In one of your earlier letters, Adrian, you mentioned Elijah. And you talked powerfully about your and Peter's childlike desire to be *good enough*. Is it possible that the hot-shot prophet blew a fuse and headed to the lonely snug of a cave, not because of Jezebel's registered letter with its death threat, but more because he never learned to cope with his own fragility? Maybe he thought that Mount Carmel marked a new stage in his life where everything was going to be sorted out – and of course it wasn't, and he was disappointed. Plenty of Christians today follow that example – dashing around the world in pursuit of the latest revival or new thing – which is inevitably a mirage. Elijah was afraid, and couldn't cope with the presence of that fear. He was devastated by his own failure. There's a little noticed line in the narrative as Elijah bleats on at God: 'I'm no better than my ancestors.' That's a telling statement, because no one ever said he should be. He wasn't superior, just called. But somewhere along the line he got the 'I'm better' idea into his skull, so when he collapsed like a mere mortal, he was devastated.

Perhaps that's when some of us Christians get into pompous, hollow piety – the 'show and tell' stuff that I alluded to earlier – the moment we start to believe that we're better. Anything good in us is surely because God has been at work making the improvements; it's grace flowing and not just sweaty effort on our part. And then, compared to God's awful holiness, (I say awful, because there's something mind-freezingly terrifying about it) we're all messed up anyway. The moment mother church takes the posture of mother superior, she's in trouble.

We're not better, just being made new. And we're on a twisted, winding path that often meanders off into a wilderness where most days can be filed under the heading 'Not much happened'. That's why I'm glad that you didn't try to talk about your dad. Whatever it is that keeps you silent, it's a relief to know that you don't feel the urge to get it all sorted out, right now. Perhaps that's for another day, or another year, or never.

I wholeheartedly agree with you about the whole forgiveness issue. Sometimes I hear Christians talking about forgiveness as if it is a Nescafe choice, an instant step.

What is true forgiveness anyway? Surely it isn't the recitation of an evangelical mantra: I forgive. I'm back to my winding pathway again – it has to be a journey, and a long hard trek at that, one that involves a series of tough choices to break the vicious circle of ungrace. Or it's like climbing another rung of the ladder, to use your metaphor. Some of the 'forgive now' urgency sounds perilously close to Nietzsche's idea that we should just shrug off our wounds, as if we are impervious to hurt. But we're not.

I even wonder if further abuse is exacted when, for example, someone who has been sexually abused is told to simply release the perpetrator. We can tell people endlessly that forgiveness is part of their healing (and it is), that God calls us to forgive (and he does) and that bitterness is a terrible poison (no doubt). But while they may express a longing to forgive (or rather, their longing to be obedient, even if the last thing they long for is to *actually* forgive) that might call for a long, honest journey, one of the two steps forward/three steps back kind.

Would you permit me just one more story about my dad? I'll make it brief.

When he escaped from that prisoner of war camp, he did so after watching some of his friends murdered, as the German guards broke their necks with rifle butts. He and the chap he escaped with worked their way through a forest and then stumbled upon a clearing, in which sat the home of a German family. The husband was away in the army, and his wife was alone with her children. Confronted by two filthy, gaunt, runaway prisoners of war, she was terrified, and feared rape and death. My dad and his friend assured her that they only wanted food, not revenge or sex, and that she and her children were quite safe. They asked for just one thing: potatoes without skins. Through their four long years of captivity, they'd been fed with potatoes with skins on. Freedom meant the luxury of the peeled version. When they left the next day, she hugged and thanked them, as if they were beloved friends. Refusing to take out their anger on her, a little step of grace was taken. But this doesn't mean that my dad was a consummate forgiver; on the contrary – he was both noble and tainted. For years after the war, he had a real problem with Italians, (having suffered badly in one of their prison camps) and would walk up to strangers in the street who just looked Italian and punch them. He was a good man and vindictive with it. He staggered on the pathway of forgiving.

And that is surely all of us. I don't understand why God the loving Father doesn't show up more, and break in, wipe tears away and send cancers packing more than he does. I don't understand the silence. My challenge is not so much that God seems inactive at times, but silent with it. It's not just the absence of intervention, but the lack of explanation that bewilders me. But I cling to this, whatever I don't understand: in my mixture and mess, in my successes and failures, in the specks of gold and the mud pools that make up me, this Father somehow loves me, and you too.

Love to Bridget,
Jeff

PS: Having started this letter by remembering Catherine Wheels and Bonfire Nights of yesterday, it has suddenly occurred to me that our happy family gatherings centred around a mock execution. With smiling faces, we sipped our hot chocolate, scoffed down our hot dogs and pretended to burn a man alive. We humans really are odd, don't you think?

EIGHT

Dear Jeff,

Thanks for your last letter, and especially the second story about your dad. I wish I could have known him. One day I will.

Also, your comments about 'self' being an irritating stain got me thinking about all sorts of things, including something that happened a couple of months ago.

Bridget and I drove up to Redhill to visit my brother Ian in hospital. He was being treated for problems with his heart, and seemed to be progressing pretty well, thank goodness, apart from enforced inactivity, made worse by the fact that he was a very large man lying on a very narrow bed, poor chap. Afterwards Bridget and I found a parking space in a street near the town centre so that I could walk two or three hundred yards down the road and pop into a shop that purported to specialise in something I needed. One of my own specialities is not being able to get things I want from places that claim to supply them. Exiting empty-handed and irritable from the shop a few moments later, and perhaps over-reacting to my failure to obtain an item that theoretically was that establishment's *raison-d'être*, I suddenly suffered a 'Lord, why can't you speak into my life more dramatically and specifically?' spasm. I get these spasms from time to time.

'Could you tell me,' I enquired sternly of the Creator of the Universe, 'how I'm ever going to get one of those thrill-a-moment testimony books written if you don't do a bit more intervening? Come on! How about something for chapter fifteen? Seriously, though,' I continued, pretending to repent of my heavy-handed sarcasm, 'it would be so nice to have some sign, some message to – you know – warm me up and send me in the right direction.'

In the far distance I spotted a woman walking towards me along the otherwise deserted pavement.

'She'll do,' I said to God. 'That woman will do nicely. A complete stranger. Why don't you get her to stop when she reaches me? She could say something significant and meaningful into my life.'

Of course, it won't happen, I told myself gloomily as the figure drew nearer and nearer. I never get to be allowed to choose when these things happen. She'll just walk past and that will be that. I'll make damn sure *that* little non-event doesn't get into my testimony book. Imagine it:

Chapter 15

God Busy Elsewhere – Nothing Happens

So firmly embedded was my Eeyore-like scepticism that when the woman really did stop dead and stare into my face, I very nearly walked on past her.

'You're Adrian Plass,' she said, her voice tinged with the faint amazement exhibited by those who discover that someone they have only heard of in the past actually exists in the flesh.

'Yes,' I replied, my whole being quivering with anticipation as I waited for her to deliver my electrifying word from the Lord, 'yes, I am.'

'We really enjoy your books,' she said, 'my family and I. So helpful. Thank you so much.'

I squirmed and issued self-effacing noises like a demented Bertie Wooster, my habitual and childish reaction to compliments, but in my head I was screaming, 'Yes, yes! What else? What have you got to say to me from God?'

Possibly detecting a slightly crazed look in my eyes, the woman produced a pleasantly neutral, disengaging smile.

'Err, well, anyway, very nice to meet you.'

And she walked on. Can you believe it? She just walked on!

'Well!' I was not pleased with the Lord of the Universe. 'That was not exactly what you might call impressive, now was it? You got the woman stopping bit exactly right, but where's the significant thingy whatsitting into my oojamaflip? Where's that, eh? Eh? Eh?'

I felt quite let down for a bit. But as the day wore on I thought about this encounter. What, if anything, had it really meant? I don't know if you've experienced this, Jeff, but every now and then I have these mental dialogues with someone or something that I can only describe with total truth and accuracy as 'the other end of the dialogue' (OEOTD). Is God in it? Don't know. Do I hope God is in it? Yes. Am I likely to know for sure this side of the grave? No, I am not. Well – whatever. This is how the dialogue went. 'M' is me, and 'O' is the other end.

O: So you weren't very happy with the outcome of your meeting with that lady?

M: No, not really, I was hoping for something a bit more meaty, more surprising, if you know what I mean. I know I get told off now and then, but over the years lots of people have told me they enjoy my books. There's nothing new about that, is there?

O: (*dryly*) No, nothing new about that. Got a bit tired of it, have you?

M: (*slightly worriedly*) What do you mean by that?

O: Adrian, some people would give their eye teeth to have what you have and do what you do. There are folks who would feed for weeks on the sort of warmly affirming comment that lady made to you. Some people might feel sufficiently warmed up by those kind words to understand that the 'right direction' (to use your own phrase) for you, is straight along the path that you are already treading. That lady, who has met you twice, once in your writings and once in person, is very important to me, and so is every other person like her.

M: So, what you're saying is –

O: Count your blessings and stop moaning.

M: (*after a little sober head-nodding*) Right. Got it. Right . . .

I felt embarrassed at that point, Jeff. I get quite obsessed by the irritating stain of my 'self' at times, and it can be disguised as a sort of spurious humility. Like the occasion when I was walking towards a venue one evening in deepest winter feeling like something that had crawled out of a dead tree after the rain.

'Lord,' I moaned, 'I honestly don't see how I can go into that building and speak to all those people about you. I've just had a row with Bridget on the phone, I haven't read the Bible for a week and I feel about as spiritual as a dead bear's bum. I'm useless!'

Cue the OEOTD. 'Now look, you can crawl into a corner and beat yourself up as much as you want. Call yourself all the names under the sun. Just sit there in a miserable lump and let self-pity soak you from head to toe. Go for it! But don't you ever, ever, *ever* despise what I do through you. Postmen smile when their feet hurt and deliver the post, they don't write the letters. Got it?'

I got it. I try to hang on to it. I lose it sometimes, like the other day in Redhill, and then I moan.

In the context of the Christian world moaning is not something we talk about a great deal, is it, Jeff? Perhaps we should. A friend of mine called Steve definitely thinks we ought to. He runs a large Christian conference centre in the west of England. One evening we relaxed together with a bottle of Hardy's Stamp in his very comfortable sitting-room, and as the evening wore on he talked with rare candour about the blessings and curses of his calling. 'I'll tell you the main problem with Christians when they stay here,' he said, filling his glass and settling into the depths of a magnificently enfolding old armchair. 'They don't get drunk, not that I've seen or know of anyway. And they don't go swearing round the place or start fights or pinch each other's stuff. None of those things are a problem. I'll tell you what they do, though. They moan. They moan and moan and moan and moan. Not all of 'em. But lots. I had a woman here the other day for instance. She found a big spider in her bathroom, or rather, it found her, rather suddenly, if you know what I mean. She said she was shocked – that was the word she used – seriously *shocked* that such a thing could be allowed to happen in a Christian establishment.' He shook his head in despair. 'I didn't know what to say.

And that's only one example. I'm fed up with the moaning, I really am.'

I sympathised with Steve, of course, and I guess there was a cosy assumption between us that we were not part of the dreadful moaning fraternity. In fact, that is not the case at all, not as far as I'm concerned anyway. I do tend to default to misery mode at times, and I probably always will because that's simply the way I'm made. However, I (both of us actually, I would guess) have so *much* to be thankful for, not least the privilege and immense pleasure of making people laugh.

In one of your letters you mentioned the person who wanted to see Jesus, instead of 'your nonsensical gibberish'. There is a gob-smacking irony about that plodding pontification. One of the most wonderfully rewarding aspects of the work you and I do is being allowed to see the spiritually therapeutic effect of 'having a good laugh'. Over the years many people have been kind enough to approach Bridget and I following an evening performance to share their relief on finding they can still laugh after a recent bereavement. One lady in New Zealand described how her father went into hospital with a terminal illness and a debilitating spiritual depression. She gave him a copy of *The Sacred Diary of Adrian Plass* to read. When I asked a little nervously what the effect of this had been, she smiled through welling tears. Her reply was sweet and simple.

'Adrian, he laughed himself to death.' In terms of ministry, how could I hope for anything more than that in this world? Laughter can be Jesus in the lives of those who dwell in shadows. It can be benevolently subversive in situations that need to be popped like balloons. It can reassure troubled souls that God is sane and sensible. It can combine smiles and tears, a cocktail of emotions that offers a little taste of heaven. It can be a Bank Holiday in the daily grind of grief and loss. It is *such* fun. Aren't we lucky to be involved in all that?

Mind you, there can be some tough nuts to crack, as you clearly know. Last year I went to a large Christian conference in the north to do an evening of extracts from a book called *Bacon Sandwiches and Salvation*. It was a tough day because I was suffering from a very nasty bout of labyrinthitis, but the session started really well. Just about everybody was laughing a lot, but there was one rather large lady, directly in front of me and in the very centre of the crowd, who greeted all my attempts to amuse with a rigidly unvarying expression of grim disapproval. I mentally christened her Bessie Braddock. Bessie's slightly unnerving lack of response continued until I reached the part of my presentation where I planned to mention an obscure tribe from the Old Testament.

'Did you know,' I queried with grave solemnity, 'that there is a tribe in the Old Testament known as the Girgashites?'

Was I mistaken, or did I detect a very slight quiver in the holy mountain that was Bessie? I spoke directly to her with slow, serious intensity.

'Imagine *being* a Girgashite.'

Bessie's whole being started to tremble gently like a volcano that seriously thinks it might like to erupt eventually. An infinitesimal twitch appeared at one corner of her mouth.

'Imagine,' I continued dreamily, 'being chased down the road by a gang of Girgashites.'

Bessie seemed to swell visibly.

'A bad attack of the Girgashites.'

Bessie hung on by the skin of her teeth.

'It sounds like some dreadful gastric disorder, doesn't it? "I've been in bed for a week with a nasty attack of the Girgashites."'

Bessie burst, rather like the enormous man in Monty Python's *The Meaning of Life* who is blown to pieces after being fed by a French waiter with one more chocolate 'wafferr'. The shreds of her hilarity exploded through the air, filling the hall and raining gently down on all and sundry.

A moment to remember.

Yes, I love the laughter, Jeff, and I thank God for it. I do enjoy the occasional moan, though . . .

Love and blessings,
Adrian

NINE

Dear Jeff,

I wasn't going to write again until your next arrives, but I feel the need to communicate with a friend. Things get very dark sometimes, don't they? Just recently I seem to have met so many people who are trudging through the darkest of dark valleys. Of course, the principle of incarnation is pretty much the only way to go when it comes to these encounters. Go down to where they are, tie their shoelaces, make them a sandwich, put an arm round their shoulders and start the climb back together. That's the Jesus way, and thank God for the pattern he set. Shouting stern advice at people through a megaphone from a very great height never did do much good. There are times, though, when the emotional effort of revisiting my personal shadowy valleys seems to strip layers of skin from any protective cover I ever had.

Answering questions with raw honesty can be very painful.

• *Do you ever experience real, total doubt, Adrian?*

Yes, I do indeed. There are times when I know for sure that the whole wobbling edifice of Christianity is just a cardboard model made badly out of cereal packets. There are times when a fundamental fear of nothingness grips me and I want to scream because the Universe has become a claustrophobic little box from which I can never escape. There are times when I wonder how I could have wasted so many years in pursuit of a ridiculous dream that can never come true. There are times when a small ball of panic rises in my gut and starts to grow larger and larger like a black snowball rolling down a nightmare mountain. There are times when all I can do is echo the words of the final verse of John Donne's wonderful poem *A Hymn to God the Father*.[3]

> I have a sin of fear, that when I've spun
> My last thread, I shall perish on the shore;
> Swear by thyself that at my death thy sun
> Shall shine as it shines now, and heretofore;
> And having done that, thou hast done.
> I have no more.

There are times when my only comfort is the comfort that Solomon offered to those who were whooping it up in the new temple when a dark cloud came down, filling the building and cancelling the celebrations. 'Don't worry,' said Solomon, 'the Lord has said that he will be in the cloud.'

And he will be. He is. He turns up.

- *Adrian, has your faith helped you through bereavement?*

Yes, but not very tidily. When my mother died, I went and sat by a lake and sent one or two anguish-fuelled shouts of 'Shit!' echoing across the surface of the water. I was glad that she wasn't struggling with her damned wheel-chair any more, and I loved the idea expressed so graph-ically in the book of Malachi that she would "come out of her stall like a young calf in the springtime", but mostly I felt angry and heartbroken and lost and alone. The human being who came closest to offering me uncondi-tional love had been snatched away. There's no way round all that stuff. No spiritual short cuts. Jesus could tell you. God just watches and waits and sheds a little tear himself. REM are right. Everybody hurts. And we're all in it together.

As I write these words, Jeff, I am reminded of a close friend of ours who lost her husband at the end of 2008. She is a truly shining example of what it can mean to fol-low Jesus, but her husband's death took all her spiritual breath away. She had been 'us', now she is 'me'. It was and is a horrible time for her.

'The trouble is, Adrian,' she said one day in a very small voice, 'there aren't any songs or choruses about things being shitty, are there?'

I had to agree with her that current editions of *Mission Praise* have little to offer in this respect, but it did occur to me that many of the psalms do actually cover this area with great passion and pungency.

'What we need,' I suggested, 'is a sort of modern psalm that will cover your very particular circumstances. I'll see if I can come up with something.'

So I did. And this is it, tailored to the tune of a rather well known song.

Greenfly on roses and flea-ridden kittens
Andrew Neil's hairstyle and dog poo in twittens
Blackheads and boils, verrucas and stings
These are a few of my least favourite things

People who chatter while cricket's on telly
Fat men exposing six inches of belly
A microwave oven that no longer pings
These are a few of my least favourite things

When the fridge stinks, when my heart sinks
When they drive me mad
Then I remember my least favourite things
And soon I feel twice as bad

Useless insurance with massive excesses
Rows of spare bog-rolls in pink woolly dresses
Cold calling crap on the phone when it rings
These are a few of my least favourite things

Times in my life that are tragic and shitty
Bloodsucking lawyers with no shred of pity
Outrageous fortune, its arrows and slings
These are a few of my least favourite things

When the car stalls, when the night falls
When I'm lost and sad
Then I remember my least favourite things
And soon I feel twice as bad

When the fridge stinks, when my heart sinks
When they drive me mad
Then I remember my least favourite things
And soon I feel twice as bad.

There we are then, Jeff. Sorry to burden you with my rant.
I guess there are times when you just want to let off steam
without the awful prospect of someone feeling the need
to fix whatever it is for you. I want to be me. I don't want

to be fixed. If God wants to make some adjustments that's absolutely fine, but in the meantime I shall be as open about the darkness as I am about the light. And if anyone objects they can take it up with Jesus, who is my model in this respect.

> Lots of love,
> Adrian

TEN

Hello Adrian,

Thanks once again for your letters. Mad travel means that I missed a round; forgive me.

I especially enjoyed the first of those two letters. How encouraged I am to know that you are also a victim of spiritual mugging. There you are, minding your own business, when bam, out of nowhere, you get slammed with an urgent need for one of those 'I need God to show up in my life more obviously then he does, and it'd be jolly nice of him to be carrying a gazillion-watt megaphone in his hand through which he'll announce something epic and startling' moments. What struck me is the suddenness of these notions; there's no warning when they hit us with the force of a rugby tackle. You're having a perfectly ordinary day, visiting your unwell brother (I hope he's better, by the way) and shopping for things unavailable (I suffer from that too, which is why I walk into shops and say 'I don't suppose you have . . .' because I actually don't suppose that they have it) and then it happens. Suddenly a major God crisis splatters all over you like a greeting from a low-flying blackbird that had a Chicken Madras last night.

Although I rarely say, 'I know how you feel' (usually those who proffer that phrase don't have the slightest clue), I think that I *do* know how you felt. I frequently get mugged. Sometimes it happens to me in Christian gatherings, which are supposed to be doubt-free zones, where one is drip-fed encouragement and strength intravenously, but where I occasionally feel like a trainee atheist. I can be perfectly happy and content one moment, and then it all goes wrong as the worship leader says something unbelievably ridiculous, some over enthusiastic person with a flag zealously tries to remove my eyes, or a fervent intercessor yells at Satan to 'Be gone!' because spiritual warfare works better if you (a) shout and (b) use Renaissance language . . .

Whack . . . in a second the mighty fortress of my faith collapses, like a sandcastle folding into brown salty slush, and I'm left wondering if belief is just other-worldly bunk. I've been mugged. And it's not so much the *depth* of the issue or question that slaps me, just the *surprise* that it can hit me so quickly. I wish these thoughts called ahead. I'd be so much happier if temptation could book an appointment. Forewarned, I could prepare.

In the case of *your* mugging, it seems that your urgent request for some instant divine input was heeded, pronto. It wasn't that God didn't say anything through that kind, lovely lady – rather it was that he didn't say anything *epic*. Perhaps we think that when God speaks, he always has to say something booming and planet-shaking, Charlton Heston style. We expect the Ten Commandments, but not a little word of encouragement. Not that I think that God is into the trivial; I heard of a church where someone stood up to share a 'prophecy' during the advent season: 'Thus says the Lord of hosts, a very happy Christmas to all my people.' While it seems unlikely that God is into sending verbal Christmas cards, it must be true that he can talk to us about small things as well as the 'important' stuff. And then again, it's very important to know that he likes us, isn't it?

In your case, it seems that God was letting you know that he loves your work – and that can be surprising too. Why do we think that God will only tell us to do something *other* than what we are already doing, which suggests that we have a lingering worry that whatever we do for him, it's not good enough. Or maybe there's something in us that is addicted to the new; change seems more spiritual (and exciting) whereas staying put is often a greater expression of faithfulness. We hanker for the shiny and fresh, which is why those air fresheners that smell of 'new car leather' are popular.

I love new things. I read those stories about Israel being commanded to leave Egypt and go on the Promised Land trek, and I wonder at their complaining; because I like adventures, I would have probably kicked up a fuss if I'd be told to stay put with the pyramids. Perhaps that's why there are some Christians who spend their lives going from church to church, on safari looking for that rarest of species, *perfectus churchimus*. If they ever managed to find it, they'd render it extinct immediately by joining it. But they continue their search, preferring a series of temporary honeymoon periods where everyone is apparently wonderful for a while (until they too are found guilty of being members of the flawed human race) rather than rolling up their sleeves and embracing the hard work of actually loving Mrs Smith who never stops talking and Mr Jones, who has to be in on everything and gets very territorial over any responsibility given to him.

Anyway, how wonderful to be encouraged as you were by that lovely lady. We all need cheering up occasionally, don't we? (Actually, I confess that I'd love to order a daily

dose of cheering up. My name is Jeff, and I'm an encouragementaholic. Perhaps most of us are.)

Thinking about those complaining Israelites, I was
interested to read your thoughts on the Christian propen-
sity towards moaning. It feels a bit strange to describe it
thus – in the USA, people don't use the word 'moaning'
to describe complaining. Our American friends, who are
generally more cheery, and believe that having a nice day
is a possibility, think that moaning is something done
during deep intercession or successful sex. The sermon
that I recently preached in the USA entitled 'Stop moaning now' therefore created some confusion and concern
among prayer warriors and newly-weds.

Some Christians have a highly developed gift of moaning, and have been practising it so long, it is practically an
art form. But what makes *Christian* moaning so very difficult to stomach is the fact that we Christians not only
moan about things in a very haughty, pious manner ('This
is not right, I'm not happy, and the God of the Universe
isn't impressed either because he agrees with me at all
times'), but most of the time we complain because we're
consummate consumers. Burger King serves us cheese-
burgers our way, and we expect Gruntsville Evangelical
Church of Christ the King to be equally compliant when
we attend its services. If the version of the Bible used isn't
to our liking, if the preacher is too long/short/amus-
ing/dry/challenging, then we suggest that the Holy
Spirit might be grieved. The truth is that the Trinity isn't
either nervous or indeed interested in most of the trivia
that niggles us. But some of us holler like rattle-deprived
infants the moment things don't suit us nicely.

So much do we like things our way, Adrian, that I've
wondered if we could create sections in our church build-
ings in the same way that we had smoking and

non-smoking areas in restaurants before that most blessed law that made freezing outlaws of all nicotine users . . .

Usher/greeter/welcome person: (*smiling*) Good morning, welcome to GECCK.

Visitor: Eh?

Usher: (*smiling more broadly*) It stands for Gruntsville Evangelical Church of Christ the King. We are delighted that you're here and, for us, when you leave our building, it will be too soon . . .

Visitor: Great. Thanks. Where do I sit?

Usher: (*smiling like the big fish in* Jaws) Well, here at GECCK, we like to do church *your* way, sir. Would you like to sit in clapping or non-clapping this morning?

Visitor: Mmm. Dunno. Anywhere else available?

Usher: (*smile fading ever so slightly only to be recovered quickly*) I'm not sure . . . we might have a couple of seats in non-listening-to-the-sermon . . .

Visitor: Right, sounds good. Look, I don't suppose you've got any room in non-clapping, non-listening to the sermon, non-participating in any way, especially the offering, have you?

Usher: (*with a crestfallen expression usually only seen at the funerals of young royals*) Oh, I'm so very sorry. That section has been booked solid for weeks . . .

We're all consumers, and what consumers do well is moan. And when we complain, the outcome that we hope for is that we are found to be in the right. That can be quite a delicious feeling . . .

I moan. I need to confess that, because your comments about complaining were very timely (that is, if being prodded in the buttocks with a sharp knitting needle is *timely*). I've just got back from yet another transatlantic flight, only to discover that I have a problem with my credit card company. We always pay our bills in time at the end of every month, because we resent paying the absurd interest rates set by racketeering banks that make the money-changers in the temple look like Sunday school teachers. (See, I was starting off on one then . . .)

Sorry. Anyway, I telephoned the company, made forty-seven selections at the invitation of a computerised woman who told me that my call was very important to her (so vital that they had a machine answer the phone), listened to some Beethoven being tapped out by a drunk with an electronic glockenspiel, only to be greeted by someone who wanted to ask me some security questions. One of them was my postcode. Normal people know their postcodes, but when I'm jet lagged I barely know my name, so I asked Kay what our code was (how am I supposed to know where I live when I'm tired?) Anyway, the chap in the call centre overheard me asking Kay our address, and the following conversation took place.

Call centre person: Excuse me, sir, I just overheard that . . .

Me: You overheard what?

C: You spoke to your wife . . .

Me: Yes, I know, that's allowed, we share a bed as well.

C: It is indeed, but you're not allowed to consult when it comes to the security questions . . .

Me: What do you mean? No one ever said I couldn't consult, where's that in the rules? I can phone a friend if I want to, the only thing that matters is that I answer the security question properly and . . .

C: But you're not allowed to ask your wife.

Me: But I'm only asking my wife because she knows the answer, and if she's not my wife, then she won't know the answer, so what on earth does it matter who I ask?

C: It's not allowed.

Me: Okay, I'm really sorry, I'll never speak to her again. Now can we sort out my problem please?

C: What's your pet's name?

Me: Eh?

C: What's your pet's name?

Me: What's that got to do with you?

C: It's another security question.

Me: Oh. It's Arnie. But I need to inform you that Arnie is dead. He expired last year after a short but painful illness. Does the fact that he's a deceased canine mean that he is technically no longer our pet, and so therefore Arnie is not the name of a *living* pet in our possession, so therefore I am technically lying in response to your question? Perhaps the question should henceforth be changed to 'What *was* your pet's name?' Or 'What's your pet's name and how is his health?'

C: I can only ask the question in the present tense, sir . . .

Me: (*wanting by now to scream a very bad word at high volume*) Oh.

C: What's your mother's maiden name?

Me: Eh?

C: It's the second security question . . .

Me: Can I ask my mother?

C: Sorry, sir, that's not allowed . . .

I fussed and fumed for a good hour after that phone conversation. But then I realised that, if God did want to say something to me and give me one of those 'moments', he'd probably have difficulty in getting a word in edge ways. So I'm going to try to do better, complain less and be grateful more.

I'd like to heed what the Bible says about thanksgiving, which is worship that is rooted in gratitude. If we wait for life to be perfectly hand-made to suit us before we'll get happy, we'll permanently postpone a smile, and ruin the best of our days.

Let's face it, when we look at a world in real need, we don't have too many problems by comparison. That shouldn't lead us to smugness or selfishness, but rather to the knowledge that Phil Collins is right: relatively speaking, this is still another day in paradise.

So how am I doing? This much is true, all things considered:

I can't complain.

> Much love to you,
> Jeff

PS: I'm writing this while in Ghent, Belgium, where I'm speaking over the weekend. This has nothing to do with anything important, Adrian, but I've just worked out that, in this city, a well-mannered chap in the loo is a gent in the Ghent gents. You see? I really am a sad person.

ELEVEN

Dear Jeff,

Greetings from one encouragementaholic to another. We're going to end up with a whole new glossary of terms at this rate, aren't we? It is true, though. A kind or affirming word does me no end of good. The other night, in the course of a tour that Bridget and I were doing with the Sailors' Society, a lady asked me if I get tired of signing books for people in the interval or at the end of the evening. I was able to reply with absolute sincerity that I never, ever weary of this particular task. Like a child who has found a barrel of sweets I simply cannot believe my good fortune. Stuff that I took out of my head a year ago and tapped onto a computer screen is actually being bought, in book form, by people who really do want to read it. It's like a miracle. I just love it. Despite being a miserable beggar at times, I am well aware that I am one of the most fortunate people in the world. I love speaking and writing, and I especially love the fact that I haven't gone to work in any conventional sense since 1984. I do work very hard (as you know, self-employed people are a strange, driven breed) but the rewards can be very sweet. Gracious and ingenious as ever, God has the Midas touch on some of my dross.

By the way, I wonder if you get asked the same things as me about writing, Jeff? I would truly love to know your answers to these questions. A few examples:

- *What if I had to choose between writing and speaking for the rest of my life, which would I go for?*

No contest, really. I love seeing people laugh and think and relax at speaking events, and I wouldn't have missed all that for the world. However, writing is something else. It is not what I do, it is what I am. Writing becomes a habit of the soul, a way of engaging and dealing with life, an antidote to the most virulent emotional poisons that one can encounter. I guess that sounds like a bit of an exaggeration, but verbal expression really does help to objectivise the (secular?) demons that can make daily living so very, very difficult at times. It can be far more positive than that, of course. There are times, not frequent, but often enough to remain alluring, when the whole thing flies like the best of two-handed kites, beauty and tension fused in the thrill of simply *being*.

Don't get me wrong. I know all about the business of searching hungrily for any and every excuse to avoid beginning the very first sentence of the day. In fact I have considerably more creativity and expertise in that area than I do in writing itself. Having said that, the answer to the original question is beyond debate. I am a writer who speaks, and if God wishes to take one of those from me, I hope and pray (although I have learned that you cannot trust God at all) that it will be the speaking.

- *Another familiar question. Does God inspire your writing?*

Well, I'll tell you something, Jeff. I've been involved in a few events involving Christian writers over the years, and I have noted a pattern. Those who sell a very limited number of books are pretty sure that God uses them as a sort of dictation facility, whereas people who write for a living and sell in relatively large quantities are not at all convinced. In one very serious sense writing is a craft like any other. We painstakingly learn how to do it, and we try to improve and hone our skills with each new project. If God is able to use the results of our labours for the benefit of his Kingdom we certainly have something to rejoice about, but I have never (with one small exception that I'll tell you about in a moment) believed that God has told me what to write about or in any way influenced the content of my books.

This may be unwitting nonsense, of course. I have already expressed my empirically-based view that God cannot be trusted. I am always asking him to be in the centre of all that I do, so he may have had more influence than I realise. If so, I am not aware of it, and, you know, I'm quite glad really. I once had my grammar and sentence construction corrected by Bishop Tom Wright (one of my theological heroes) when we were sitting side by side doing a radio programme together. That was bad enough without Almighty God chipping in with his slightly more omniscient views on correct use of the semicolon.

The exception? Ah, yes. Well, I'm talking about the opening story in a collection called *The Visit*, one of the first things I ever wrote. It dealt with the arrival of 'The Founder' (clearly intended to be Jesus) at an ordinary high street church in the mid-1980s. Was it genuinely an exception? I don't know. I do know that Bridget and I will never forget how dramatically that short piece came into existence.

We were at home one evening doing nothing in particular, when the opening words of a story simply filled my
mind. Panicking slightly, I asked Bridget to quickly find
paper and a pen so that I could dictate. It was truly
strange. The story unfolded without any pause. Words
tumbled from me. I wept as I dictated. Bridget wept as
she wrote. We seemed to be carried on a wave of pure
passion that could only be dealt with by allowing it to
land where it wished.

It swept through me like a flood and hardly a word has
been changed since the moment on that evening when
Bridget laid down her pen. Despite faults in the style and
construction of the story, it embodies a raw power and
passion that twenty years of writing have not equipped
me to repeat at will.

Interestingly, Jeff, there was an odd aspect to the writing of one other part of *The Visit*. I was recovering from a
stress illness at the time. Probably the story I was telling
was a misty reflection of my own recent history. I think –
I am sure – I was trying to write Jesus back into my life,
and it seemed to be working. Then an obstacle arose. I
was halfway through the fifth section, but found myself
unable to complete it. In this part of the book the main
character, horrified by what he has done, has decided to
run away. Unable to sleep, he crouches miserably all
night beside a suitcase in the hall of his home, waiting for
the dawn.

Suddenly, unexpectedly, The Founder has come. He is
outside the front door, calling urgently to be admitted.
Unable to face such an encounter, the wretched man turns
to see a dark figure waiting beside the open kitchen door,
apparently offering him a way of escape. He must choose.

That was as far as I had got, and the atmosphere in our
house that evening was dark and weighted, like the

lowering calm before a storm. Bridget begged me to finish the story so that light could return to our lives. Reluctantly I did that. The character in the story made his choice, the right one I trust, and the darkness lifted as if a wand had been waved.

I cannot explain this bizarre experience. It simply happened. I guess that on a level I don't comprehend an important decision had to be made, and I was part of it. God knows the rest. By the way, you may be interested to know that my main character made his peace with Jesus in the end.

- *Another oft-repeated question: Which of your own books or pieces of writing do you like best?*

One answer is always true. The book I happen to be working on at the moment is the most important and all-absorbing thing I have ever written. I think it has to be like that for me: until the next time. When the dust has settled between books, however, I think the response to that question might surprise some people.

There are certain poems I have written that are short, verbal snapshots of very specific moments in my life. Why these brief happenings should be charged with such intense significance is not easy to understand, even for me. All I can say is that freezing time and emotion in this way affords me an immense amount of satisfaction, even if the resulting pieces don't do a great deal for anyone else. Here is one example, written last year when Bridget and I were taking a break in the north of England. The title is almost as long as the poem.

**A little girl picks up a stick on the path down to High Force
    waterfall in Cumbria**
At first she thought it might be something good to eat
But found it slightly sharp when she touched it to her lips
Perhaps a pencil, hold it like a pencil
No, no point
No point
A thing you wave towards the sky?
Yes!
Fallen from a tree
A thing that waves towards the sky
Glance at some internal clock
Quick! Time to skip
Drop the stick forever
On to see the waterfall, whatever that might be
On the path the stick lies still and stick-like
Totally fulfilled

The second example is something that I thought I would
never perform or read aloud because, although special to
me, it seems to be about nothing at all. I was a bit embarrassed, I suppose. When I did recite it at some conference
or other, I was quite taken aback by the rapt attention
with which it was received. Thinking about this afterwards, I concluded that people identified with a reminder
of the strange, mountainous, inner intensity of the *ordinary*, rather than with the poem itself. Weird, isn't it?

Someone I knew
I was sitting in a café on my own
Someone I knew walked past the window
Someone I knew!
There!
Just walking past the window

Someone I knew and who knew me
Walking past the plate-glass window!
So – how to handle it
I worried that if I left my place the waiter would not
    understand
He might remove my coffee and my garlic bread
He might think that I had left
I went anyway
Tried to signal that I would be back
I doubt he understood or noticed
I hurried out and caught the person that I knew
I said hello, so did he, then he walked on
It was just someone I knew.

- *A final question: If God doesn't tell you what to write, where
  do your ideas come from?*

Easy! Everywhere. Everyone. At all times and in all
places. In joy, sadness, illness, danger, serenity, there simply is no location, time or condition that is inherently
incapable of inspiring some kind of idea for use in the
future. I recorded in an early book the occasion when
three of my children and myself fell out of a boat on a
fast-moving river, and I was trapped under the capsized
boat with no knowledge of how I would survive or what
was happening to my two sons and one daughter. In
addition to all the normal panic, fear and confusion, I
have to confess that a little voice in the back of my mind
was calmly suggesting, 'This will make a very interesting
article if you get out alive.'
    Loony or what!
    Nowadays I keep a file on my computer labelled
'IDEAS'. Every idea, good, bad, half-baked, important or
obscure is farmed from the backs of envelopes and stored

away in case it's needed in the future. These things are too valuable to be lost, especially when your memory is as dreadful as mine. I *lu-u-u-rve* my IDEAS file.

I'd really like to know how you view your writing career, Jeff. You moved from being a speaker to being a speaker who writes, didn't you? I travelled in the opposite direction, but we seem to have met in the middle.

Lots of love,
Adrian

TWELVE

Dear Adrian,

I am so delighted to hear how much you enjoy book signings. I love them, but have battled a niggling feeling that I'm just enjoying being a slightly large goldfish in the tiny bowl of celebrity that is the Christian world. Truthfully, I don't think that's really why I love sitting at that table, pen in hand. And there is a challenging side to them. Book signing sessions can be a nightmare, especially at the beginning of a writing career. You park yourself behind a table in the strategic epicentre of a bookshop, and sit in the shadow of what seems like a skyscraper of books – books *you've* written, the towering pile of paper a sobering monument to the fact that they are, as yet, unsold.

You wait, hopeful, praying that some kindly browser will take pity on you and (a) help reduce the stack that eclipses you and (b) ask you to sign the book they buy. Not fun, particularly when they pick up the aforementioned tome, take ten minutes to scan it, then sniff, slap it back down on top of the undiminished pile and walk away.

But I do love book signings because of the incredible people I meet. I've discovered that anonymous superheroes sometimes stand in line for a squiggle of ink. Do you try to write something different for each person, Adrian? It can feel very strange – and pressured – when someone says 'Give me a word from God' at a book signing, as if I am a chocolate vending machine ready and waiting to dispense a life-altering message in a shiny wrapper. Not only does this imply that the God of the Universe is just standing on tiptoe waiting to download to me a witty, prophetically incisive comment for the next person in the queue, but I also wonder whether this is the charismatic equivalent of popping off to see Mystic Meg.

Besides, I'm usually the one who learns a lot about God at book signings, because of some of the remarkable people who show up. Remembering some of the book signings I have experienced has made me grateful again, Adrian, for the gift of laughter. I love the total commitment that full-on laughter demands; a belly laugh is like a physical and emotional mugging. Your shoulders shake, your eyes close, there might be a few tears, and some people (especially ladies of a certain age) even wet their knickers a little. You can't talk while laughing, and you certainly can't complain, yell, or be unkind. But what we can do is learn while laughing; when we laugh at a punchline, it's because there's been a connection; an idea has been proposed, and we got it. Not that I want to justify laughter on the basis of it being 'helpful', which is like saying that a gorgeous rainbow is 'useful' because it helps the ozone layer (it doesn't, I just made that up). The rainbow is beautiful because it is, and laughter is the same.

I'm still pondering your questions about whether I prefer speaking to writing, and I think I'd have to say speaking, because of the immediacy of it. I'm there when that person smiles, sheds a tear of relief, or nudges their friend to make sure that they got the point. It's up close and personal. I love to write, but I can't be there when the light goes on in someone's eyes, or even when they throw the book across the room because I've niggled their religious sensitivities. (Perhaps that is a good thing. A very attractive lady came up to me and said that she enjoys my writing, and always takes me to the toilet with her.) And writing is a lonely business. So if I had to make the choice, I'd probably opt for speaking.

As for the question, 'Does God inspire your writing?' – however I answer that question, it will be wrong. If I say 'No', then what's the point of me tapping away at my laptop, if I don't believe he speaks through me? And if I say 'Yes', then I risk claiming something that sounds grand and pretentious – there are too many Christian writers already who think that every sentence they compose comes straight from heaven. So perhaps I'll just play it safe and say 'I hope so.'

My best book? I actually like the writing I did in a book called *Creating a Prodigal-friendly Church*.[4] I worked very hard indeed at crafting the words and researching the background. I think it's my best writing. Sadly, only about thirty-five people – including members of my family – have read it.

And my ideas? I am fascinated by human beings. I watch. I listen. I study my own disposition. Here's a question for you. As a preacher turned writer, I'd like to ask you: what do you think about those who say that preaching has had its day? And what kind of preaching have you found helpful? I am assuming that there is some that has been . . .

With much love to you Adrian,
Jeff

THIRTEEN

Dear Jeff,

Thank you for your last letter, and particularly for the question at the end about preaching. It sparked all kinds of memories and reflections. Before I mention one or two of those, however, let me add just one more anecdote to the book signing canon.

Three or four years ago, I travelled to Hungary for the first time. I was a little apprehensive. Speaking through an interpreter you have never met before to an audience who may decide within a minute and a half that you are mad, theologically unsound or boring is challenging. Fortunately, my interpreter was charming and competent, and the predominantly youthful men and women who came to the meetings were bright-eyed with anticipation. Most of them had read *The Sacred Diary of Adrian Plass* (in Hungarian!?!?!?) and they seemed keen to feast their eyes and ears on the British lunatic who had written it.

As the first meeting ended, I assumed that I would complete the evening by signing a few copies of a newly translated book. I was wrong. To my surprise and mystification, I actually signed more books on that occasion than at any other time before or since in any other part of the world, including the United Kingdom. It went on and on and on as a seemingly never-ending line of people snaked its way slowly past the little table where I sat with my patient interpreter. It was all very satisfying and flattering, but the trouble with me is that I have a tendency to get tired and say stupid things.

Digressing, I remember, for instance, making a complete idiot of myself at a gathering in Newcastle. I was signing books in the entrance foyer of the church before the meeting began, when a lady approached me with the following words.

'Would you please sign this for my friend Eileen, only she's – you know – inside.'

Weary from a week of bleating and travelling, I put very little energy or intelligence into processing this sentence. I pictured the aforementioned Eileen, sitting miserably in some Holloway cell, waiting and hoping for the gloom of her wretched situation to be illuminated by the divine torchlight of my immortal words. These are the precise immortal words with which I inscribed the flyleaf of her book.

'May you be free – even in that place . . .'

Eileen's friend took the book back and gazed with furrowed brow for a few seconds at the words I had written.

'No,' she said, looking up at me dispassionately, 'I meant she's inside the church. She's saving me a seat.'

I was horribly embarrassed, but later, after being in the church for a while, it did occur to me that my message might have been appropriate after all . . .

Anyway, back to Hungary. Two thirds of the lengthy queue had passed my little table and gone away with their signed books. It was a real joy to see such enthusiasm, but I was beginning to feel exhausted and slightly dizzy from the repetitive nature of my task. There was something strangely unreal about this tiny capsule of a world in which I smiled and signed my name over and over again without a pause. I decided to break into the pattern.

'And what is your name?' I brightly asked the next young lady who presented her book to be inscribed.

She told me her name, but to my untutored English ear it sounded like a collection of random syllables.

'Ah,' I replied, feigning interest, but genuinely wanting to be friendly, 'and what does your name mean?'

My interpreter passed on the question in Hungarian, and received an answer.

'She tells us that her name is also the name of a certain flower that opens and closes at night.'

'Well, how lovely,' I drivelled on mindlessly, 'and are you like that flower? Do you also open and close at night?'

My interpreter, tired after a long day, automatically began her translation, but I noticed that her voice slowed and faltered as she neared the end of the sentence. A rather dank silence fell upon the three of us. In my head I was re-running the question I had asked and wishing that I could die, my translator was gazing sadly into the distance and probably praying that my wish would be granted, and the girl named after a flower that opens and closes at night was moving her mouth soundlessly.

What is there to say when, in front of a large gathering of fresh young Christian folk you have accidentally come out with a vaguely smutty, innuendo-ridden question that doesn't even really make any sense? Well, there is the option of blathering on wildly in an attempt to make things all right. Not a wise course of action when everything has to be translated into Hungarian and back again. Or you can just smile in a grown-up, you-may-have-detected-something-unsavoury-in-what-I-just-said-but-I-never-notice-such-things sort of way, and move swiftly on. That's what I did. On I went. Swiftly.

Okay, Jeff, you asked about preaching. I'll tell you about the worst and the best that I've heard. The former is easy. The worst I've heard was me, preaching in the ancient chapel of a very famous college in a very famous university somewhere in Great Britain. It was near the beginning of my speaking career, and I was simply overwhelmed and personally threatened by the grandeur and formality of the environment in which I found myself. It was pathetic. I was pathetic. Instead of being myself and speaking with the freedom that they had hoped for, I turned into a boring pedant, my spindly ego intimidated and crushed by the weight of history and scholarship surrounding me.

Since that day I have learned two golden rules about speaking to groups of people. The first is never to adapt, and the second is always to adapt. Never adapt in the sense of trying to become somebody else. They don't ask somebody else. They ask me. Within those parameters I am always ready to adapt to features and nuances pertaining to the people I meet and the situations in which I find myself. It can make all the difference.

I was once speaking at a chapel service in a young offenders' prison in the Midlands. There was a lot of messing about and poor behaviour as the time for my talk drew closer and closer. For a lot of these young men, chapel was nothing more than a chance to get out of their cells for an hour or so. The actual content of the meeting was of little interest. A number had already been removed because they had played up so outrageously. How would this crowd react when I got up to speak? I was not relishing the prospect.

When I did finally get up and walk to the front I realised that, even in the midst of this confusion and uncertainty, my mind was filled with thoughts about my daughter Kate, a brand new, amazing gift from God. I had only known her for two weeks. How could I be missing her so intensely? Arriving at the lectern I turned to look at my congregation. They looked back, their flaccid body language and lazy-eyed, scornful expressions eloquently declaring that I might as well not bother.

The opening lines of my planned talk drifted away from the front of my mind. What could I possibly say that would have the slightest impact?

'I'm really missing my daughter...'

You could have heard a feather drop, Jeff. They were all really missing someone. In their minds each one of those lost lads was seeing distant, inaccessible faces and places that meant the world to them. They knew exactly what I was talking about. And it was all right after that.

'There you are,' whispered a voice in my mind as I travelled home on the train later that day. 'That's the way to go. Start from where you are, not where you think you ought to be.'

The best preaching I have ever heard? I'm not quite sure what 'best' means in this context, Jeff, but I can tell you about the talk that had more of an immediate impact on me than any other. Having said that, there is no trace in my memory of either the text that was preached on, nor any single scrap of detail from the content.

It happened in Tunbridge Wells, the town where I grew up, and where, at St. John's Church, I became a Christian (not quite sure what that means any more) at the age of sixteen. A year or so after my conversion it was announced that a speaker from an organisation called the Fountain Trust was coming to address an open meeting in

Tunbridge Wells. It was all very exciting. Fountain Trust featured strongly in a growing charismatic movement that had already spread through an unprecedentedly wide variety of church denominations. The speaker, a man called Edgar Trout, was reputed to be a great man of God. What would happen at his meeting? We younger ones loved all the fireworks of the charismatic movement, even if we pretended they were secondary to more solemn and worthy aspects of the faith. Perhaps this Edgar Trout man would let off a few spiritual bangers and Catherine Wheels and rockets in the course of the evening. Couldn't wait!

There were no fireworks. Not a one. Not so much as the humblest, least impressive little fizzer that gets taken out of the box and lit carelessly after all the decent ones have been admired and enjoyed. Indeed, at first it all looked disappointing in every way. As the vicar rose to open the meeting I stared at the somewhat shabbily dressed, not very impressive looking man sitting quietly in a chair waiting to be introduced, and wondered if I might be about to waste an evening. There was just nothing about this man that inspired confidence. He was sort of – well, brown. Ah well, ninety minutes of boredom and then we could nip round to the pub for half an hour.

The vicar concluded his opening remarks and Edgar Trout rose to his feet.

The room filled up with God.

No fireworks, nothing as impermanent and superficial as that, just light, heat, presence, a dynamic reminder or reassurance that the material world really can pulsate with the beating heart of ultimate truth. Words fail me. The problem with looking so far back into the past is that memories of memories take over from genuine recollection. All I can tell you for sure, Jeff, is that the memory of

Edgar Trout's visit has fed my soul for more than forty years. Does it count as preaching? Don't know. Don't care. Doesn't matter.

In closing, I would just like to add a word about a lady called Brenda. Brenda is married to Malcolm, and both are of retirement age. A couple of weeks ago Bridget and I were touring with Saltmine Theatre Company (great people, and well known to you, I believe), and it was Brenda who prepared our food one evening and generally looked after us. They were a wonderful couple, those two. They will never write Christian books or appear on platforms or express revolutionary, complicated views on the knottier aspects of Christian theology, but, in the best and most genuine sense, they've cracked it. They do it. They are the real deal. If authentic humility, a willingness to serve without reward and a hardworking day-by-day commitment to following Jesus are what Christianity is all about, then I suggest that all the training colleges and Bible schools and seminaries and writers and thinkers and theologians should organise coach parties to the house where Brenda and Malcolm live out the faith that we all spend so much time talking about. Brenda and Malcolm would be a bit surprised, but Jesus wouldn't. He lives there as well.

I can see it now. Brenda will pop the kettle on, Malcolm will nip down the road for extra biscuits and Jesus will watch with some amusement as all these intense seekers after truth begin to realise that the last really, really *will* be the first – in his eyes, anyway. Want a good sermon? Go and see Brenda.

God bless, Jeff,
Adrian

FOURTEEN

Dear Adrian,

I laughed out loud when I read about your marvellously inept moment when you were chatting with the Hungarian 'flower' girl. Part of my laughter comes from relief. I'm heartened to know that there is at least one other person on planet Earth who loves Jesus and is as stupid as me; well, almost. And I empathised as you described that rather strange but wonderful twilight zone that is a book signing. Whenever I am bone-weary (which is often), or around a lot of people (also a frequent happening), the likelihood that I'll place both of my size elevens firmly in my mouth is huge. Sometimes it's just that in trying to say *something*, one blunders into saying something so gob-smackingly inept that angels probably scratch their heads in disbelief . . .

I was speaking at a certain Christian event recently when a young lady came up to have a word with me after an evening celebration. It's easy to sense nervousness in people, isn't it, Adrian? As she approached, I could see that she was a little flustered. Wondering if she had some awkward confession to make, or was just bothered at having to approach a stranger, I made a decision in a millisecond to try to put her at ease.

'Hello!' I said jauntily and, noticing that she was wearing a T-shirt with lettering on the front, I decided for some insane reason to try to use that as a conversation starter.

'So then, what does your T-shirt say?' Instantly her face fell and then turned beetroot red. I thought that she had perhaps purchased her fashion item from one of those 'Christian' T-shirt places, with some kind of slogan on the front, like 'Rapture Ready', (which sounds like one is in need of a truss); 'Don't get caught dead without Jesus'; 'Be patient, God isn't finished with me yet' or even the subtle 'Will you miss the abyss?'

But evidently this particular T-shirt was *not* purchased from The Living Word in the High Street, because the lettering that marched across her more than ample bosom luridly and fluorescently proclaimed, 'Oy you, stop looking at my boobs.' The fact that we were chatting together in a large tent meant that my very next flustered comment was almost 'It's so good to see you in the Big Top', but helpfully, I bit my tongue just in time.

Your agony was heightened because you were working with a (longsuffering) translator, who obviously was on a mission from God to help you out. I've preached with translators quite a lot, and when it comes to humour, it can be quite a challenge, don't you find? Some time ago I spent four days teaching at a conference attended by Christian refugees from Sri Lanka. Held in Paris, every word at the conference was translated into Tamil, which is one of those languages where one word in English, like 'Hi', is followed by about two or three minutes of translation. Anyway, I was telling some of my 'funny' stories, and noticed that those lovely people seemed to be really enjoying them. They guffawed and giggled and sometimes collectively roared with laughter. I was encouraged that my humour was translating across the cultures. Half way through the third day (which had been especially hilarious), I turned to the translator mid-session and remarked that I was so pleased that the funny stuff was working, and how interesting it was that my Sri Lankan friends 'got it'.

'Actually, they don't get it at all, Jeff. Every time you say something amusing, I say to them, "Jeff was just funny again. Please laugh now."' And those delightful, kind souls did exactly that. Rather than offend or discourage me, they pretended to be side-splittingly amused. A bit like your smiling friends, Brenda and Malcolm, they were gracious, and although I was one very unfunny preacher, they laughed out of loving kindness.

I sometimes hear people talking about revival. I think we need something of a revival of kindness in the church. Kind people 'preach' the best, sometimes without words. I learned that a few weeks ago, when I did a little book tour with a man called Gram Seed. I don't know if you've come across Gram. He's a northerner, his real name is Graham, but, as he says, 'My Nana called me Gram, and it stuck.'

Gram is one of the most gentle people I've ever met, which is a surprise, because he has spent half of his life behind prison bars. A giant hulk of a man, he has muscles in places where I don't even have places. His life has been a battle with terrible addiction to an evil trinity of violence, drugs and booze. As a member of the Middlesborough 'Frontline' (a group of hardcore football hooligans), he used to trudge around the nation and organise locations for fight-to-the-finish battles with other football 'supporters'. His body has been broken by those bloodlettings; his face slashed with a Stanley knife and the side of his head caved in with an axe. He looks like a club bouncer who has spent decades on the door. Gram ended up homeless and lived on a park bench for three years, until finally he became very ill, fell into a coma, and was set to die. His mother was called into the hospital to sign the relevant forms so that the life-support machine could be turned off.

To cut a long and marvellous story short, a group of Christian lads who had been talking to Gram in the park about Jesus (despite him repeatedly telling them to go away with a repeated common phrase, the second word of which is *off*), showed up at the hospital and asked permission to pray with him before the switch was thrown and his life ended. They prayed, he woke up, and some weeks later became a Christian. He now spends his life going into prisons (as a speaker, not an inmate) talking to young offenders about God. Just as you captured the attention of that restless and disinterested crowd when you said, 'I really miss my daughter', so Gram is able to powerfully talk about the marvellous love of Jesus that has totally changed his life, because he's been where his listeners are. And he's managed to avoid becoming too Christianly Christian, if that makes sense?

Anyway, back to the aforementioned book tour. Gram and I were speaking at a church event somewhere in the UK (I won't mention where it was, in case any of our readers come from Manchester), and we were not having a good day. The hotel where we were staying was horrid. It was dirty, smelly and when we checked in, the receptionist asked if we wanted a room with a window, seeing as that would involve an extra charge. But the ants in the windowless room were thrown in for free.

We came out of Fawlty Towers to find that our car had been decorated with a parking ticket. This was not a good day. Fleeing through the rain to a local pizza place for lunch, we sat down at our table, feeling rather glum, our mood mirroring the dreary weather. The waitress arrived.

During the meal, Adrian, we did absolutely nothing at all that would have advertised that we are Christians. We weren't wearing T-shirts with 'snappy' slogans, and we wore no fish or dove badges. We didn't say grace before eating, sing a hymn, and when it comes to tambourines, we weren't carrying any. At the end of the meal, the waitress gave us the bill, and, chatty and friendly, asked what our plans were for the rest of the day.

'Are you going shopping, lads?' she smiled.

We replied that, no, we weren't here for retail therapy, but rather were in town for an event that evening.

'Is it about God?' she asked. We were shocked, and replied that it was indeed an event about God, and asked her how she knew.

'It's simple', she said. 'You were nice to me. I get a lot of horrible people in here, a lot of complaining and abuse. But you boys were nice. I figured that it probably had something to do with God.' We came out there wide-eyed, amazed at the prophetic power of a little warmth and kindness.

Kindness is also linked to this matter of the best and worst preaching that we've been discussing. You said that the worst sermon you ever heard was delivered by you; and one of the best by kindly Brenda. Perhaps unsurprisingly, I'm a little mortified to confess that the All Time Most Terrible talk in my hearing was one that was delivered by me. It was when I first started preaching many years ago – but don't read too much into that last statement. Some Christian leaders only talk about their gaffes and sins in the past tense, as if their foibles are only ever part of very ancient history. I, however, have a catalogue of far more contemporary failures, and I'm sure I've preached a few duds very recently.

This sermon of mine was breathtakingly inept. Knowing that I was about to go to Bible college for ministry training, the minister of our church arranged for me to be the guest speaker at a nearby chapel. It was a crumbling little building that housed a tiny congregation. Without being ageist, one or two of them were so advanced in years that I fear they may actually have been dead, propped up in the pews, faithful but rigid. Certainly they didn't move, react or obviously breathe at any time during my stunningly awful message. If they *were* dead, I'm so glad for them, because they were spared the drivel that came out of my mouth. My sermon had three points. Brace yourself, Adrian, hold onto something solid, because you are about to be stunned by the amazing wisdom that flowed that day. Not.

Point number one: *Christians don't have problems.*

Point number two: *If you do have problems, pray about them, and they'll go away.*

And the epic finale was the clincher, Adrian, the pearl of truth that must have made the living members of the congregation feel that they were indeed swine:

Point number three: *If you have problems, and you have prayed about them, and they haven't gone away, then you are probably not a Christian, which is a very big problem indeed.*

I know, Adrian. It deserves an award. It makes me to preaching what the Cheeky Girls are to music. But here I return to the power of kindness, because the members of that church who were still sporting a pulse were absolutely lovely to me. They thanked me for coming, very gently encouraged me to study, and showed beautiful grace by just sitting there and enduring the oratorical equivalent of a root canal operation. I preached utter rubbish, and they responded with mercy and blessing. I still marvel today when I think of it.

Thirty-five years later, I'm still preaching. I sometimes preach five times in a weekend (at Timberline Church, where I'm a teaching pastor, we have eight services; I preach the same message repeatedly, with the same outline, illustrations, and spontaneous humour). I recently told Kay that I preach so much, I get sick of the sound of my own voice. She said that she understood completely how I feel.

But having come back from yet another preaching tour yesterday Adrian, I have to tell you that right now I'm not praying that I'll be a better preacher, but that I'll be a kinder person. Standing up and delivering a talk is relatively easy. But as I discovered only yesterday (I told you that some of my sins are very recent), it's a lot harder to be nice when the day is boring and people are inept. Our car started to go wrong yesterday; the steering lock was coming on at very strange times, which is unhelpful and dangerous unless you plan to drive in a perfectly straight line. We called a dealership and asked for their service department, and were told that if we took a considerable detour out of our way then a mechanic could take a look for us. We were misinformed. When we arrived (having been given the wrong directions), we were told that they were too busy to help us, and that we should call the RAC and ask them to transport us home.

I didn't shout, rant or punch anybody. But I did do more than my fair share of huffing and puffing, and I could certainly have been kinder and more pleasant in the face of irritation. An honest mistake had been made. I, who had been shown such grace when I preached such a duff sermon (and have been shown plenty of grace ever since), was unwilling yesterday to pass that grace around. Muttering came easier, hence my prayer that God will help and change me.

So have yourself a lovely day. With all of the afore-mentioned chat about kindness in mind, it's worth saying this, and I mean it: I'm grateful for you, and for your friendship.

      With much love,

        Jeff

FIFTEEN

Dear Jeff,

I nearly wet myself (I am open to any unconventional baptismal experiences) over your account of the Sri Lankan interpreter. How on earth did you continue after learning that your listeners were laughing out of charity? I fear and worry that, in your position, I might have defaulted, as a number of Christian speakers do, to guilt-inducement and cataclysmic prophecy of imminent disaster as a means of regaining control and self-respect. As you know I love using humour, but it really can be tricky at times, can't it?

One of the things I least enjoy is what you might call *encouraging* laughter. I was in a Baptist church on a Saturday night a couple of years ago where the organiser clearly felt that his paying guests were not responding enthusiastically enough to my cherished little gems. He began to produce hideously loud, rhythmically mechanical guffaws that were obviously intended to indicate and inspire amusement. He actually sounded like some sad soul who has been threatened with torture if he fails to find MFI flat-pack assembly instructions hilariously funny. So bizarre and unearthly were these clockwork cachinnations that the attention of my audience was almost exclusively drawn to the individual who was producing them. I suppose sudden madness and car crashes have the same effect. Everybody looks. It went on to be a less than successful evening.

I agree with you about kindness, Jeff. When all else fails, kindness will usually succeed. The waitress who served you and Gram (I'd love to meet Gram one day, by the way) evidently saw the kindness of God in the way the two of you responded to her, just as the person who let you down over the car did not. Please don't think I'm judging you, Jeff. On the contrary, your experience is a depressing reminder of something that happened to me in a motorway services car park last year. Easier to preach than to be kind? Yes, that just about sums it up. This is what happened.

Bridget and I parked and I got out of the car. As Bridget tried to get out on the driver's side her door knocked quite gently on the door of a blue car parked next to ours. Almost immediately a small, irascible man with a grey beard appeared from nowhere, and launched a fierce and quite personal attack on Bridget, barking loudly about the car being a very expensive one, and allowing her no space to apologise or defend herself or indeed to say anything at all. My wife is more ready to apologise than just about anyone else I know, even when she hasn't done anything wrong, but this fellow simply wasn't listening. At this point I decided that enough was enough, and I began to point out that, whatever damage had been done (none, as it transpired) there was no need or reason to be rude and offensive. So far so good, eh, Jeff? I couldn't let the man go on shouting at Bridget like that. But then the son arrived, spitting with anger, pointing out that it was his car, and that his father could not have been the slightest bit rude, because he was not that sort of person. We should be ashamed of ourselves, added his mother, who had also materialised from somewhere.

'Do you not think,' I said, 'that it might have been better for your father to have restrained himself a little and allowed my wife to apologise and offer to pay for any damage?'

'Oh, and that's what you would have done if I'd bashed my door into yours, is it?' he asked, thrusting his face into mine.

'Well, yes,' I replied, 'I'm pretty sure that's exactly what I would have done. I'd have smiled and said, 'whoops!"'

'Well, I find that pompous and patronising!' he retorted.

Suddenly I saw red, but it was a chilled, tightly controlled sort of red. I didn't care a jot for him or his father or his mother or their eternal souls. All I wanted was to win, and having encountered this man for a minute or so I thought I knew how to do it. The tone of my voice when I spoke was one of calm, frozen, totally dismissive contempt.

'Try not to be so silly.'

And I turned away towards the restaurant.

He pushed his body round in front of me, his face only inches from mine. He was almost frothing at the mouth with rage. If he was going to take a swing at me it would be now. But mother stepped in.

'Leave them,' she said, 'come away, they're not worth it!'

When we returned to the car later there was a small dent in the back that had definitely not been there before. We climbed into our vehicle, and just as we were about to pull out of our space, a van drew up beside us. Turning off his engine, the driver opened his door, accidentally knocking it into ours in the process. Bridget and I looked at each other and burst into laughter simultaneously. The driver, who must have thought we were slightly deranged, gestured apologetically from the other side of the window. I smiled back.

'Whoops!' I mouthed.

The bit I regret about all this is that for a short space of time I not only cared nothing for those people and for the younger man in particular, but I actively and viciously wanted to do harm to him. I suppose I could have called over my shoulder as I turned away, 'Do you want to make a commitment?' but somehow I don't think it would have carried much weight.

These things happen, and they do cause me discomfort. The revelation of what we become when we are cornered can be quite disturbing. The shameful, wonderful fact, though, is that we can be forgiven; shameful because we are reminded again and again that the righteousness is not ours, and there are times when we Christians hate to be reminded of that, and wonderful because it is the free and willing forgiveness of a fatherly God that will bring us safely home one day.

By the way, the other thing in your last epistle that made me laugh and grit my teeth was the account of that early sermon. Oh dear. How I wish I could have been there, Jeff. Three points all beginning with 'C' and probably ending with 'P'. I bet you preached with total conviction and rock-like assurance. That's what we do when the fact that we know next to nothing is a secret that has not yet been revealed to us, isn't it? Don't worry. You are not alone. I too exercised a powerful Ministry of Discouragement at one stage in my life, mainly on the streets and in the cafés of Tunbridge Wells. It was as if Jesus' command to me had been: 'Go out into all the world, particularly at a time when all the world is busy with something genuinely important, and put them off following me because they don't want to become an insensitive, arrogant git like you.'

So what has changed? Having finally grasped the inescapable fact of my own ignorance, why don't I just shut up? An interesting question, Jeff. I suppose the broad answer is that passion has replaced certainty, although the former can quite often be mistaken for the latter.

One example of this. A couple of years ago Bridget and I were responsible for the ministry slot during a holiday festival week at Carberry Towers near Edinburgh, one of our favourite conference centres, and a place where we invariably meet lots of old friends. Guests found it a difficult week for all sorts of unexpected practical reasons, but the atmosphere was very positive, and we really did put a lot of feeling and thought into attempting to make our morning sessions as relaxing and accessible as possible. On the last day of the festival I was walking back to the accommodation block where our room was situated, when I encountered a little girl. About eight years of age, she was a daughter of the worship leader and his wife, a charming couple who had produced a whole tribe of those vivid, characterful children that you could cheerfully sit and watch all day. As I stopped to greet her, this dark-haired, still-spirited one gazed up at my face, fixing me with a knowing eye.

'You,' she said with solemn gravitas, 'know a lot about God, don't you?'

I can't remember the words I used in reply, hopefully something neutral, friendly and harmless, but I do remember the sudden, silent, panic-stricken cry that rose inside me like a dark fountain, addressed to her and to anyone else who might feel the same. I take that bloke Ortberg's point, but I can hardly handle the boat, let alone

get out and walk on the water. I'm a doubter and a wor-
rier and a shifter of my ground. I'm needy and fragile and
sometimes lost. I pray and I hope and I rage and I continually entreat God to fill my battered soul with sweet
peace. So don't tell me, don't anyone tell me that I know
a lot about God, because if it's really true that I'm the one
who knows and you're the ones who don't – well, my
brothers and sisters, we are in big, big trouble. On a thousand different occasions, standing outside a thousand different sets of garage doors, I have said these or similar
words to the God who inhabits my passion, my pain and
my puzzlement:

Have mercy, Lord, have mercy, I'm weary to the core,
It must be someone else's turn to stand up and be sure.

I'm afraid it all sounds a bit dramatic and overstated, does-
n't it? But it is the truth about my reaction, and of course it
begs a question, the question that I have already asked.
Why do it at all? What are the vital elements of this passion
that is more powerful than knowledge and more strangely
inevitable than a dfs sale? The answer to that question is
probably true for both of us. Jesus is the answer. He is the
reason, the motivation, the heart, the light that blazes like a
floodlight or flickers like a birthday cake candle in the
breeze, but is never actually extinguished. It is my yearning for him, my deep-down wish that all should be well
between us that fuels my desire to continue communicat-
ing and encouraging and challenging and making space
for those who are on the same strange journey as me. It is,
I hope, a reflection of his frequently expressed, over-
whelming desire that we should look after each other.

Jerome K. Jerome would understand that small hope of
mine. Here is one of my favourite moments from *Three*

Men in a Boat, his wonderful celebration of ordinary humanity.

> We feel so helpless and so little in the great stillness, when the dark trees rustle in the night-wind. There are so many ghosts about, and their silent sighs make us feel so sad. Let us gather together in the great cities, and light huge bonfires of a million gas-jets, and shout and sing together, and feel brave.[5]

That may not be a conventional picture of evangelical Christian gatherings, but it will do for me. I sometimes wonder, Jeff, what Jesus thought about as he hung, feeling profoundly abandoned, on that cross. All sorts of unfathomable things no doubt, but perhaps there were flashes, fleeting images of Sabbath walks meandering through rolling fields of wheat, the chattering and chuckling of his friends, their sweet naivety, a scent of cooking fish, the call to eat, old stories by the fire, beloved faces in the night, lit by heat and happiness. If only he could be there, bathed in familiar, glorious ordinariness. He couldn't, of course. He had already turned down the Twelve Legions of Angels option, precisely because he wanted future generations to enjoy the re-creation of that rich sense of togetherness with him. And, in the end, that may be at the very core of what I do. It might sound a bit low-key, but I just want to be part of organising get-togethers with Jesus.

> God bless you, Jeff,
> Adrian

SIXTEEN

Hello Adrian,

You asked how I coped when I knew that my Sri Lankan friends were laughing on cue. I just carried on, because that is what we Christians often do, regardless of whether anyone is listening or we are being offensive and unfunny. I've been to a few Christian gatherings where the people leading paid absolutely no attention to their audience/congregation. But I suppose that I was really able to carry on because I knew that these people were so utterly kind, they were willing to guffaw to order just to keep me happy. Their graciousness enabled me to continue, (red-faced, I admit) until the event was over.

Your words about ordinary humanity in general, and your chat with the little girl at the conference centre who thought that you were 'special', have nudged my single brain cell into gear. I have come to the conclusion that we need to celebrate the ordinary more, and dust down the mundane and welcome it with open arms. As I write this, I am listening to a tape of a highly convincing and indeed authentically sincere preacher who wants me to believe that I can single-handedly change the world by next Thursday afternoon, and that Jesus has made me into a sort of superhero. He informs me that I can do all things through Christ who strengthens me, which of course is not true in the way that he is putting it, because I cannot play the bassoon, understand Sanskrit or take the lead male dance role in the Nutcracker Suite, although I must confess that dashing around in a codpiece looks like a lot of fun. The bassoon never appealed.

To me, one of the most wonderful things about Jesus is that he is both remarkable and splendidly ordinary at the same time. Perhaps that's why I get niggled and huff and puff at those artists who have painted the nativity in such unreal hues, with Mary dressed from head to foot as a blue nun (unusual kit for giving birth), and a baby Jesus (complete with a junior sized halo) who is surrounded by grinning, perfectly behaved farm animals, including worshipful sheep who are baaing their praises. In these paintings, baby Jesus is sitting up already, which is quite remarkable seeing as he is only twenty minutes old, and is looking lovingly at the donkey that stands smiling, despite being without a carrot, to his left. It looks as if our junior Lord is about to address the Wise Men, and thank them very much indeed for showing up at his birthday party. Joseph is not usually seen in these portrayals, Adrian. One assumes that he is off somewhere fixing a wonky coffee table, or that he just doesn't have a fluorescent enough glow to make an appearance. What frustrates me about the *airbrushed* nativity is that the fabulous ordinariness of the occasion is obscured. Even the writer of one of my favourite carols, *Away in a Manger*, meandered into this blatant unreality

> The cattle are lowing, the baby awakes
> But little Lord Jesus no crying He makes.

Why on earth wouldn't Jesus cry? I imagine that, if I was born in a stinking shed with a herd of lowing bovines (whatever lowing is) and then had a bunch of strange mystics show up with obscure gifts like gold, frankincense and myrrh, but without a chocolate bar or a Pooh Bear sleep suit or anything made by Fisher Price in sight, I'd be tempted to scream the place down, and make a big mess in my swaddling cloths. Of course, a newborn wouldn't be aware of any of these things, but you get my point. The mind-bending wonder of it all is that the eternal Son of God became a crying baby, and not a miniaturised intergalactic visitor.

And then there are those who, terrified that they will rob Jesus of his divinity by emphasising his humanity, object strongly to the idea that the Son of God went to the toilet while on this planet. Going to the loo is one of the most basic components of ordinary life; we all do it frequently, and those who don't buy bran and wish that they did. But there are those – believe me, I've met them – who insist that Jesus didn't vacate his bowels for a whole thirty-three years. The thought of the King of Kings parked on a more ordinary throne appals some beyond belief. This ludicrous idea is not only foolish, but is in fact heresy. Docetism is the false notion that Jesus was not really human, but only appeared human. The truth is that Jesus was fully man, and therefore did all the ordinary stuff of life.

But I'm especially glad that the commitment to the ordinary continued even after Jesus' resurrection. The beauty and the glory of it is in that it *is* unspectacular. If I'd been asked to choreograph the resurrection, it would have all been very different. Think Cecil B DeMille meets Steven Spielberg. I'd have brought the Red Arrows in, and they would have provided a fly-past scrawling, 'Jesus is risen, so in yer faces, Pharisees' in blue smoke in the sky. I'd have had eleven thousand angels tap dancing on the beach in yellow Doc Martens, with the London Philharmonic Orchestra and a Welsh male voice choir. It would have been arresting and unforgettable, and would surely have cheered the disciples up no end.

But the resurrection minus my event management skills is nothing like that. There's no Jesus caught in the flash bulbs of the paparazzi. Instead, he gets mistaken for a pottering gardener. He goes for a seven mile stroll to Emmaus with a hapless couple who are heading in entirely the wrong direction.

And then he goes fishing and does a little shopping and cooking – or so it appears. When Jesus cooked breakfast for Peter and his other pals, he got the fish and bread from somewhere, didn't he? I suppose there might be some who think that our Lord just whispered 'Hovis', or the Aramaic equivalent thereof, (Jehovis) and the bread just appeared, ready sliced. The same people would imagine that Jesus then approached the lapping waves on the beach and yelled, 'Haddock, come forth' whereupon a couple of pre-filleted fish just flew out of the sea and landed in his hand, all ready to cook and with a nice lemon and thyme topping. I'm more inclined to think that he went fishing or shopping. It's all very mundane. And we lose the glory of that when we try to sprinkle it with glitter.

You and I both live lives that are quite varied and exciting, but even with that said, there are still lots of times for me that could be filed under the heading of 'Not much happened.' But Jesus is still with us in the ordinary, uneventful and plain boring bits of life that are part of the human deal.

So why am I banging on about this? It's because sometimes I fear that Christians advertise an experience that isn't terribly authentic. If we advertise something on the can but it's not true, then we'll set people up for disappointment and crisis of faith. But it's not really a crisis of real faith – just faith as advertised and promoted by us.

That's why I think we must avoid the temptation to dress up our experience of faith and make it just a tad more spectacular than it really is. Last week I heard a speaker who recounted a happy little chat with the Holy Spirit that went on for about fifteen minutes, back and forth. I seriously wondered if it happened that way, or whether shorthand language was being used to describe a mental journey, but the shorthand suggested an ease of relationship that is not quite real. I don't know about you, Adrian, but I am never sure about whether God is speaking to me, even after being a Christian for over thirty-five years. At times I am unable to tell the difference between the voice of the eternal God and the meanderings of my own imagination. And to those who point to the happy chats that the Almighty had with various folks in the Old Testament, I would want to remind them that sometimes there were many years of silence between these dramatic encounters. We don't do God or God's people any favours when we insist that faith is about skipping from one dramatic, epic moment to another.

Perhaps that's one of the reasons that you and I both enjoy recounting our most embarrassing moments, Adrian. Not only do they make people smile (hopefully), but they illustrate this truth: in the midst of the ordinary, everyday fumbling of life, and the red-faced *faux-pas* that you and I seem destined to continually make, God is. And that cheers me up no end. How about you?

By the way, I've decided that next time I write, I'm going to tell you about one of my experiences that still brings a rush of embarrassed blood to my face whenever I think of it. But I think perhaps I'll let you go first. Any massive gaffes on your part lately?

With much love,
Jeff

SEVENTEEN

Dear Jeff,

Any gaffes on my part? Need you ask? Since writing a while ago about my hideous experience in Hungary, I've been thinking about all sorts of embarrassing things that have punctuated my wretched life like a plague of exclamation marks. One that springs easily to mind is my last visit to Marks and Spencer to buy a pair of trousers.

Bridget buys most of my trousers on-line nowadays. There are two reasons for this. First of all, the M&S on-line facility seems to stock a much greater selection of trousers in my size, whereas the stores themselves stock a range suitable for immensely fat dwarves or emaciated Masai warriors. Hence the second reason. I hate and loathe and detest the whole business of trying on badly fitting trousers in those cardboard thin, coffin-sized cubicles with the flimsy curtains that only meet the door frame at one side, however hard you try to twitch them across at both ends. I feel hot and heavy and red-faced and fat and murderous from the moment I step inside these ghastly little hell-holes.

On this occasion I was trying on a pair of jeans that must, despite the measurements on the label, have been specifically designed for a circus clown whose right foot has been amputated. Having mountaineered down into the vast denim basin at the top of this ludicrous garment, I managed to get my left leg in and through the appropriate aperture, but was unable to find a hole at the bottom of the other leg for my right foot to penetrate. The struggle to maintain my balance involved an increasingly rapid hopping movement on my left leg, with the half-trousered right leg gyrating wildly in the air as I desperately tried to locate the hole that surely, *surely* must be there somewhere.

The inevitable happened. The inevitable usually does happen to me. I lost my balance and fell backwards, limbs flailing, and crashed into the wooden side of the compartment with such planet-shaking force that I feared the whole line of cubicles might collapse behind me like a pack of cards, leaving me lying on my back for the whole of Marks and Spencers to see, half inserted into my clown jeans and with one imprisoned leg waving helplessly in the air.

This total collapse didn't actually happen, thank goodness, but it was bad enough simply emerging sheepishly from my cubicle a couple of minutes later, aware of troubled, surreptitious glances from nearby shoppers and sales assistants who must have listened to my impression of a disgruntled rhinoceros trapped in an MFI wardrobe with alarm and puzzlement. I was *so* embarrassed.

No more buying in the store. Not ever. I've made my mind up. It's going to be on-line shopping from now on.

My in-store shopping catastrophes pale into insignificance, however, when set against an experience so blood-curdlingly dreadful that it causes my blood to run hot and cold whenever I think about it. I should add, Jeff, that your view of my sanity may have radically changed by the time you finish reading this bizarre little anecdote (assuming you think I'm sane at the moment).

I have to begin by begging for your acquiescence in the notion that we all have funny little habits and preoccupations that might seem a trifle odd to the rest of the world. I have a few. Please tell me you have one or two yourself, otherwise I shall feel like the man in Monty Python who asks, 'Which of us can honestly say that we have never burned down some great public building?'

One of my little habits is balancing things on my head. Yes, that's right. I sometimes like to balance things on my head. Have a titter by all means, but it's not all that funny really. It's simply that I rather enjoy the physical stillness that is imposed on my body by balancing, say, a small occasional table or a pint glass half filled with water on my head. Something to do with the endless search for true serenity? Perhaps. Oh, all right – I'm bonkers. It is also true, I have to confess, that I do relish those moments when an unsuspecting member of my family walks into the room to discover me performing an even more extreme balancing act than they are accustomed to.

So, there I was sitting in the kitchen one morning, watching some rubbish on the television, and hoping that Bridget would walk into the room soon. I was looking forward to witnessing that pungent mixture of amusement and exasperation on her face as she encountered my latest balancing extravaganza. On this occasion, though I say it myself, I really was pushing the limits. On the top of my head sat a very large china plate, and in the absolute centre of this quite expensive item of tableware stood an uncorked wine bottle half-filled with J.P. Chenet Cabernet Syrah.

All would have been well if I had not forgotten an arrangement made earlier in the week with a handyman named Alec, a competent, simple soul who lived locally. He was due to come round that morning to work out an estimate for laying a patio in the section of our garden visible from the kitchen window. Aware of a movement of some kind outside the window, I swivelled my eyeballs, obviously with meticulous care so as not to disturb my head furniture, to see Alec, metal ruler in one hand and notebook in the other, standing stock-still and staring anxiously through the window in my direction.

It was one of those eternal moments, Jeff. As my swivelling eyeballs met his paralysed ones, there was an instant of true surrealism, a sort of Surrealistic Happening, in fact. It was as though George Ormerod, my wife's Lancastrian father, a lifetime devotee to moderation, had opened his front door expecting the man who delivered vegetables, only to find Salvador Dali twirling his mustachios on the step and offering pictures of melting clocks for sale.

After two or three seconds, Alec turned abruptly away and began busily to measure the nearest thing he could find. But you will understand that the damage was done. Our relationship could never be the same again. From his point of view, I had been revealed as an insane person who sat alone in kitchens, solemnly, inexplicably balancing plates and wine bottles on his head. From my point of view, Alec was a man who would carry that revelation into every single encounter we might have in the future.

The incident was never mentioned, neither by myself nor by Alec. But every word that passed between us from that day onwards was eclipsed by and saturated with a silent conversation that was never actually going to happen.

'Why were you balancing a plate and a wine bottle on your head in the kitchen? Why were you doing that? Why?'

'Look, I want you to know that I am not mad. I am not mad. I'm really, really, *really* not mad. I can see how it looked, it looked as though I was mad, but I am not. I was balancing those things on my head because – well, because – er, I like doing it . . .'

'So you are mad.'

No, that conversation was definitely not going to happen. Every time I think about it, I feel *so* embarrassed.

Interestingly, a major negative feature of the stress illness I mentioned in a previous letter was a loss of embarrassment in such apparently unimportant areas as the dropping of litter. I was brought up to regard this (together with such enormities as the audible passing of wind) as a sin almost on a par with arson or armed robbery. Small children are somehow able to accept and absorb this kind of unequal distribution of moral weight. I remember reading somewhere about a class of junior aged children who were asked to list the worst crimes you could commit. One child had placed 'Murder' at the top of his list, with 'Running in the corridors' in second place. Common sense takes over as you get older, of course, but the child inside never quite abandons these templates. Consequently, at the age of thirty-six, even in my disturbed state, I was horrified to find that I was able to throw a sweet wrapper on the ground without feeling any sense of guilt or shame. Minuscule as this might appear in comparison with some of the other things I was doing (I'll tell you about them one of these days, Jeff), it was, for me, a significant measure of the distance between the individual I had been, and the dislocated personality that was now being endured by those close to me.

What it boils down to, I suppose, Jeff, is that, leaving aside lunatics who ricochet around changing rooms or balance stuff on their heads, embarrassment is a necessary component of civilised community living, a brake or check on behaviours that are not appropriate or helpful. I seem to remember from some psychology course I did a million years ago that embarrassment is reckoned to be a product of role conflict. In other words, it happens when one or both sides of a relationship neglect or deliberately depart from the role that has previously maintained stability or peace.

One of these days we might have the chance to meet Adam and Eve. Opinions vary on that topic, but if we do, I suspect that they will have something fascinating to say on this particular subject. What do you think?

God bless,

Adrian

EIGHTEEN

Dear Adrian,

Thanks for yours. Your stark confession about your hobby of balancing things on your head not only made me laugh (and I had a go myself with a small table lamp, which I never liked anyway) but has emboldened me to share an agonising incident from my own inept little life. This one has never made it into print before, and I've only recently started talking about it in public. Prepare yourself, Adrian, because on the few occasions that I have mentioned this episode, people have reacted by giving me that wrinkled-nosed expression usually reserved for those who make bad smells in public.

Let me ease you into this by first telling you about the runner-up in my 'gaffes of a lifetime' list. It happened at yet another one of those Christian events involving chalets (I sometimes think that hell may involve chalets). Our family was much younger then; Kay, Kelly and Richard were fast asleep, and I had to be up at the crack of dawn for one of those early morning prayer meetings (you know, where we haul ourselves out of bed and sit around for half an hour in a warm room fighting sleep and mumbling, 'mmm' and 'Amen' every few minutes just to let our fellow sufferers know that we're still semi-conscious). I decided in a mad moment to dash from our bedroom to the bathroom while naked; I didn't want to take a dressing gown into the damp cell that was the bathroom, and so decided to make the short trek through the living room (onto which the front door opened) in a state of utter undress.

I got halfway across the room, when suddenly I heard the terrifying sound of a key rattling in the front door, and realised that someone was on their way in. It was the cleaning lady. The door swung wide and a cheery lady with a broad smile popped her head round the door. I froze to the spot, one buck-naked Christian without so much as a pocket New Testament to maintain modesty. And the strangest thing happened, Adrian. She looked me right in the eye (for which I was most grateful), and then seemed to pretend that absolutely nothing was amiss. I expected a scream, a muttered comment about coming back later, followed by a bustling retreat or even an expletive or two and an accusation that I was a pervert, but none of this happened. Instead, she acted as if chatting with a naked stranger was a very normal part of her day, and then asked me a totally unanticipated question:

'Would you like me to hoover your carpet?'

So utterly gob-smacked was I by this, that I looked around the room to see if the carpet did indeed require the attention of a vacuum cleaner. My screaming urge to do a back flip over the kitchen counter and retrieve a spatula with which to cover my nakedness was suspended. She treated me normally, so I acted as if nothing was wrong with our totally bizarre conversation. It was only a few moments later, after she wished me a good day and left, that the extremity of the situation caused me to break out into an embarrassed sweat.

But this pales into insignificance compared with what I am now going to share with you, Adrian. The episode in question doesn't have any comic value, and it wasn't embarrassing at the time. It's just recalling it that makes me feel so weird, even freak like.

I've mentioned my dad before. He and my mum were good, hard-working parents who were incredibly busy. Perhaps it was a generational thing (my dad's father was a kind but quite stern Victorian type) but there wasn't much conversation to be had when I was growing up. My brother left home and emigrated when I was twelve, and so from that time on I was effectively an only child. I can remember feeling a tangible sense of loneliness; I had some good friends at school, but always felt on the outside, under a terrible pressure every day to perform and fit in. I was heading towards angst-fuelled teenage years when I would be the first to get out-of-my-head drunk at parties, because I would pour a mixture of whisky, gin and vodka into a half pint glass and drink it down in a few seconds. I was almost instantly incapacitated and nauseous; looking back on it, it's amazing that I didn't kill myself with the shock of alcohol poisoning.

Anyway, back to me as an eight-year-old, or thereabouts. I remember the day that our house was burgled. It was quite a chaotic scene. Drawers were pulled out, their contents roughly scattered all over the place; furniture was turned over and vases and chintzy ornaments toppled. Strangely, nothing was actually taken; it all looked as if the thieves had gone in search of something valuable, had given up after trawling through our stuff and had fled. The police were summoned, and as I had been the one who discovered the break-in, I had to give a statement. Looking back now, I wonder about the kindly constable who patiently took notes as I told of my shock at coming downstairs to discover the mess. I think he knew the identity of the burglar.

I think he knew that the primary suspect's name was Jeff.

It was me, Adrian.

I turned my own house over. I staged a mock burglary.

I was so desperate for someone to just notice me, to talk to me, that I resorted to transforming my own home into a crime scene. I remember spending a good half hour with that patient PC. He listened attentively as I made up a description of the man that didn't exist that I 'saw' running out of our house. I think I must have been fairly imaginative with my photofit profile, and thankfully didn't tell him that this fantasy criminal was wearing a stripy jumper, a bandit mask and carrying a bag over his shoulder that was emblazoned with the word 'swag'.

I'm almost sure the policeman knew. But, quite wonderfully, he listened to my woven fabrications, assured me that I would be safe because the burglar probably wouldn't come back as he had found nothing of value, and gave me much more than the time of day. To this day the minor crime probably remains as a technically unsolved case, Adrian. Perhaps, because he knew, PC Kindness didn't even bother to file a report. To do so might have risked me getting into trouble for wasting police time.

But the local cop and the hoover-brandishing cleaning lady did the same thing; in abnormal situations – meeting a naked chap and a terribly lonely kid – they treated me as normal. They didn't try to sort me out or fix me.

Sometimes, I wish we Christians would do more of just that. Perhaps it's all done with good intentions, but we followers of Jesus can become holy meddlers on a crusade to sort people out. We (who are so unsorted ourselves) can be quick on the draw with 'answers' which are little more than slogans; instead of just shutting up and listening, we rush to dispense our sometimes silly solutions. I see this in both the tragic and the trivial. An example from tragedy first. Just yesterday I met a delightful couple who lost their fifteen-year-old son to a brain tumour last year. The pain of his death has obviously been excruciating, but they confessed that it's been made worse at times by 'helpful' comments from Christians, who've come dashing in to try to roughly dry their tears and tidy up their lives with answers that aren't answers at all.

They've been told that they need to trust Jesus, the one who gives and takes away, and who therefore is the one who took their boy. But Jesus didn't 'take' their son, did he? He doesn't use death to kidnap people because he needs a bit more company in heaven. It was cancer, a wicked tumour that took their boy. Some people told them that they should be happy, because their lovely boy is now with Jesus. But that's exactly the problem, isn't it? They don't want their boy to be with Jesus, or anywhere else, no matter how palatial the accommodation; they want him to be with *them*. Then there's the 'It was his time' comment, as if God is the bloke who runs the dodgems and then calls you in when he thinks you've had more than your fair share of fun. But the 'time's up' idea doesn't really work at the funeral of a fifteen-year-old, does it? Ask the parents of a still-born child and they'll surely tell you it works even less for them. Their much-awaited darling didn't even get to start the ride. There are no reasons that we can give to grieving parents that are going to make the slightest difference to how devastated they feel. I won't even give space here to the insanely daft notion that someone died because of someone else's faith, or lack of it. My writing will become shrill and this letter will become even more of a rant.

And then there's an example from utter triviality.

I'm on Facebook, the on-line community where people can tell each other that they are going for a walk, or are constipated, together with other stupendously dull updates. Recently I made a little joke on my Facebook page about seagulls. I was speaking at an event where there were enough manically vocal gulls to provide the extras for Hitchcock's *The Birds*, and they looked equally evil too. Having spent nearly three weeks in their shrill company, I posted a little tongue in cheek comment on the day of my departure:

Jeff is thinking of leaving a little something for the seagulls to remember him by. Like a hand grenade.

Suddenly my Facebook page was littered with twittering complaints from Christians who urged me to consider that 'Jesus loves the seagulls as much as me' (an interesting notion that I won't mess with here, but this must mean that our Lord also has great affection for tsetse flies, man-eating anacondas and the chicken I ate for lunch yesterday), and calling on me to repent for my anti-gull comments. Not only does this confirm my suspicion that some Christians have had a sense of humour by-pass, but it also worries me that, once again, the believing brigade come screaming round with blue lights flashing to spray us all with gallons of correction fluid the moment we utter something suspect.

I know that the Bible encourages us to nudge and even rebuke each other so that we won't be caught in insane and life-vandalising sins; but surely that doesn't mean that today is yet another opportunity to run around looking for people to sort out, pronto. Sometimes, surely we need to just offer a reassuring smile, or just listen, so that other people don't become like the 'prompt' person in the corner of the stage, feeding us an opportunity to open our mouths and say yet more verbiage. Okay, enough for now.

> Much love,
> Jeff

NINETEEN

Hello Jeff,

Do you know the television programme called *The Secret Millionaire*? I think most countries have their own version nowadays. In each episode a multi-millionaire goes under cover for a couple of weeks in a deprived area, with a view to giving away thousands of pounds of their own money to deserving causes at the end of their stay. Of course, the presence of a camera crew has to be explained away somehow, but that never seems to be much of a problem. Leaving aside the uncomfortable awareness that my emotions are probably being expertly manipulated by the programme makers, I always find it a very moving thing to watch. The featured projects and enterprises are invariably run by genuine, humble people who are working hard to make a difference in very difficult circumstances, and their astonishment on being presented with such huge and unexpected financial windfalls appears unfeigned.

Last night as I watched the latest in the series, a few words spoken at the end of the programme struck me very forcibly. They came from one of two men who run a boxing club in Northern Ireland for lads who might otherwise be getting into all sorts of trouble on the streets of Belfast. On being handed a cheque that would make it possible to find new and more appropriate premises for the club, this fellow looked into the camera lens with an expression of shocked incomprehension on his face, and said the following words:

'You think you're alone – but you're not!'

I've been thinking about that ever since, and particularly about the fact that this man's experience is precisely what so many Christians (and non-Christians) long for. Not the money exactly, but the stunning immediacy of God sweeping benevolently into their lives to prove that they are not alone, that he does care, and that he really can make a significant difference to the situation they find themselves in. It's a little bit like the policeman you mentioned who so generously offered grace instead of law at a moment when you needed it most.

Experience suggests that if I were to say this publicly I would be pretty swiftly buttonholed and reminded or informed that this is exactly what God does do when men and women ask Jesus into their lives. So what on earth am I talking about? Well, whatever anyone says, it really is not as simple as that, is it? Let's suppose that someone were to ask you or I the following very simple questions:

'What should I expect to happen when I become a Christian? What will God actually do? How will I feel? What will change?'

When I think of the Christians I've known and the stories they have been good enough to share with me, I have to accept that there are all sorts of answers to that query. A few examples.

Nothing. That's what happens to quite a lot of people. Jesus suggests in the parable of the Prodigal Son that the Father will throw his arms around sons and daughters who return home, shower them with gifts and throw a party to celebrate their homecoming. And yet many people who would call themselves Christians have never experienced this explosive encounter. They have experienced nothing. Nothing at all. Leaving aside the trivial little fact that, in the most important way of all, they may have been granted eternal life and total forgiveness, there is no actual evidence to suggest that God is any more or less present than he was before the prayer was prayed or the commitment made. Two or three generations of nervous preachers and evangelists have somehow managed to turn this deficiency into a virtue.

'You don't have to worry,' they burble optimistically. 'It's a good thing really. You see, quite a lot of people don't actually experience anything at the time. It's a matter of faith, you see. Trust God and the future will bring all sorts of blessings. Take a step into the darkness. There'll be light on the other side. You'll see!'

Sometimes this prediction is absolutely spot on. The future does bring real, perceptible blessings, but them sometimes it doesn't. Why is that? Answers on a postcard please.

For other new converts the answer is that *every* blessed thing happens. They speak in tongues. They prophesy. They enjoy a powerful sense of God being with them, filling body and soul with a knowledge of his love and care. They fall off their horses on the road to Damascus, hear Jesus talking to them, go blind, get healed and end up taking the gospel to the Gentiles. I have a friend, once a frighteningly dangerous, violent man, who knelt down in the cell of his high security prison and asked God to change his life. At that moment and from that day onwards, his life was transfigured. He was a new man. A wonderful, old-fashioned, tin-tabernacle miracle. Fantastic for those who begin their Christian lives with such dramatic encounters. Puzzling and a little intimidating for those who don't.

Some people would deny that they ever crossed an identifiable spiritual starting line. Perhaps they grew up in a Christian family where being a follower of Jesus seemed as natural and inevitable as breathing, and in most cases their faith appears no less genuine for that.

At least two people I know became Christians primarily through fear. I hope and pray that they have subsequently learned something about the love that has fought so bravely to dispel our dread of being lost in the Universe, but there is no doubt that the threat of hell brought these folk to repentance in the first place. No problem with that really, I suppose. Jesus was very strong on the subject. Perhaps the reason so few people switch on to the good news is that they have never been helped to comprehend the bad news. I know that the concept of hell is not too fashionable in some quarters of the church nowadays, Jeff, but I would respectfully suggest that those who embrace this view should check that God has managed to keep up with contemporary theological thinking. He can be a bit slow and obtuse sometimes.

I've only mentioned four possibilities for those who want to know how God will greet them when they turn to him. There are many, many others. Why the differences? Why doesn't God issue an identical emotional and spiritual starter-pack to every convert just to reassure them that they're on the right track? Sidestepping from the responsibility of answering such a difficult question, I can only offer a couple of reflections, Jeff. I would be very interested to know your response to these ideas.

First of all, I would suggest, as I hinted in a previous letter, that some conversions are not conversions at all. One of my favourite writers is Paul Tournier, a Swiss doctor who spent years counselling Christians in trouble. Stepping into the world of his relaxed, compassionate wisdom is like dropping into a gently bubbling hot tub at the end of a wearying day. He quietly explained to one of his patients that it was almost certainly the nature of his so-called conversion that was choking general growth and the specific development of peace in his life. Evangelical Christians find this sort of thing very difficult to accept, of course. Conversion is a significant component of the 'Being a Christian' kit, and it seems like a sort of heresy even to question the validity of such a sacred event. However, as we all know, life simply is not like that. For instance, some returning prodigals seem to get hi-jacked before they ever reach the Father. I wrote the following words years and years ago:

The Prodigal Son abandons his job with the pigs, just as in the parable, and sets off towards his father's house, nervous about his reception, but determined to go anyway. Not long after the start of this journey he is intercepted on the road by an enthusiastic but deluded individual who has heard only a distorted account of the father's habit of forgiveness. This man doesn't *quite* believe in what he's heard, but he thinks he does, and he'll feel a lot happier when he's not alone.

'Hi!' he greets the trudging penitent. 'Good news - you've been forgiven!'

'Great,' says the Prodigal.

'Here you are,' says the deluded one, and he wraps an imaginary cloak around the lad's shoulders. He mimes putting a ring on his finger. Together they sit down to eat a non-existent fatted calf with invisible knives and forks.

'Isn't it wonderful?' he enthuses.

'Oh, yes!' responds the Prodigal, intensely relieved that he is to be forgiven so impersonally and painlessly. 'Yes, it is!'

They meet regularly for mime sessions. A group forms. Everyone becomes very proficient at mime. Time passes. At last our hero feels bound to express his growing concern.

'The er . . . cloak and the ring and the calf – they're not actually real, are they?'

His lack of faith is rebuked and disciplined. How dare he spoil the game for others. He feels guilty and unhappy. Common sense tells him that the things are not really there, and he doesn't actually feel forgiven. One crucial question. Where is the father?

Eventually, either he settles for the troubled half-life of tediously repetitive mime sessions, or he goes back to the pigs, or, if he's got any sense and he's had a session with someone like Paul Tournier, he leaves his mime instructor behind, dumps his meaningless conversion and moves on up the road to risk a genuine encounter with his father, who is anxiously awaiting him with a real cloak, and a real ring, and a real fatted calf.

And real forgiveness . . .

In case this scenario seems far-fetched and not genuinely applicable to the church, it is worth noting that the Sailors' Society (previously known as The British and International Sailors Society) began in the nineteenth century after one of its founders spotted a notice outside a church that read 'No Sailors or Prostitutes.' We, as a worldwide church, are still dealing with a legacy of intolerance and Phariseeism from these sniffily respectable little mime organisations and, even worse, we are allowing new ones to develop. The difference, of course, is that the new ones have, consciously or unconsciously, mastered the art of miming Spirit-filled Christianity so effectively that it is almost impossible to tell the genuine from the false.

So, there's one reflection. Sticking the 'conversion' label on to some experience or other doesn't necessarily mean anything. You can unstick it. You might need to. God will help you. You might feel a jolly sight better afterwards.

Then there's the whole thing about individual differences. A few months ago I made the mistake of tuning
into one of those blow-wave evangelists who stride up
and down platforms in wildly expensive suits, trumpet-
ing the most mundane spiritual truths as though they
hadn't existed in the Bible until they discovered them last
Tuesday, and leaving long dramatic pauses that don't
mean or do anything at all other than invite applause,
and getting docile congregations to repeat dismal little
half-arsed mantras like parrots to each other and – oh,
don't get me started!

Anyway, this particular character said something that
made me want to burst through the television screen and
strangle him with his own Italian silk tie – just to show
him that I understood more about the love of God than he
did, if you get my drift. These were his words, delivered
in the solemn, soupily pedagogic, Thatcherite tones of
one who is telling us something we need to know for our
own good, even though we might not like it:

'The only thing in you that God loves is Jesus . . .'

What a horrible thing to say. What a sad and inexplicable denial of all that life and the Bible teaches about God's
very individual, caring relationships with his people. The
Prodigal Son. Peter. John. Cornelius. David. Jonah. Jacob.
Elijah. Me. You. Brenda. Malcolm. The list would have to
go on until we have included every single person who, in
the entire history of the world, ever interacted with the
living, loving, bewildering, vulnerable God.

So, if I discover it really is true that the only thing that
God loves in me is Jesus, I might take out a subscription
to my local wombat-worshipping assembly and seek ful-
filment there. As I think I said when I wrote before, each
of us is different, and those differences, loved and
respected by a God who knows from experience exactly

how it feels to be a human being, are bound to affect the way in which we approach and perceive the invitation that he extends. Thus, for people who have been badly hurt and betrayed in relationships with those who should have been looking after them, it may take years or even a lifetime for the process of being born again to be completed. As we all know, every church has its little contingent of these folk who patently never quite manage the 'spiritual stuff' that's supposed to happen. Jeff, when will people realise that they are not warts on the Body of Christ? They are not bad adverts for what we believe. They may be difficult, and they may sometimes be burdensome, but they *are* the Body of Christ.

The quick-fix merchants can say what they like about this. Miraculous change does sometimes occur, but the fact remains that many Christians are so broken up inside by negative circumstances and cruelty suffered in the past that they can only survive through years of love, attention and practical concern from believers who are fortunate enough to have a little stability and charity to spare and share. And let's be honest, they may have to go on sharing in this way until the moment when the two of them walk arm in arm through the gates of heaven as equals, and Jesus smilingly congratulates them both on making it.

So that's the second reflection. Individual differences. They can make all the difference.

I could go on and on, but it would become even more boring. And, in the final analysis, of course, I have to confess that I am not privy to God's motivation in allowing or causing such wildly varying experiences of himself to those who reach out to receive his love. Who knows what is going on behind the scenes? Who knows what battles have to be fought, what devilish manoeuvres have to be thwarted, how much darkness has to be dispelled so that Emily Dunworthy of 16, Dibley Road, Penge can reach a point where she thinks she might have a sort of feeling that she has possibly experienced a tentative sense of the reality of God?

I suspect that the Holy Spirit is a divine opportunist when it comes to drawing in the objects of his passion, and perhaps that is the most important consideration in the end. However we came to faith, no matter how disappointingly uneventful or excitingly dramatic the experience may have been, we are facing in the right direction, we are in the right company, and the best is yet to come.

How will it come? Well, I guess the major frustration attached to the whole business of deciding to 'become a Christian' is exactly the same as the one involved in getting married or moving to a new house. However carefully you may plan and prepare for change, the fact remains that spending your life with another person or living in an unfamiliar home means very little until you are actually doing it. Christianity is not an event. It's a life, a decision, a confused but benevolent entanglement.

Jeff, I am as confused by the whole business as I ever was, but the old glow of excitement inside has never been extinguished, and it still prompts me to say to non-believers and troubled believers alike, more or less the same words as that man said on the millionaire programme:

'You think you're alone, but you're not.'

God bless,

Adrian

TWENTY

Dear Adrian,

Okay, I really must complain. It seems to me that our letter writing has hitherto been a warm and enjoyable experience; one that might well get us both into hot water, but nevertheless an engaging exchange, at least for the two of us. But your last letter totally ruined all that! Adrian, what are you thinking? Have you been too long at the foamy Harvey's trough?

Your last epistle, with its question about why some people seem to have daily theophanic encounters with the Almighty as part of their usual routine, while others apparently have little or even *nothing* happen to them at all, has got under my skin, niggling at me like a pesky mosquito attempting a crash landing in my right ear, and has hijacked my brain and heart ever since I read it. Even this morning's shower, a normally relaxing time when I sometimes sing tuneless praises to God (which he probably doesn't want to hear – my new album, *Songs the Lord Rejected*, is out soon, available at a tasteless Christian bookshop near you), was totally hijacked by your question; my brain was turning over and over like an ancient washing machine clogged with twenty pairs of water-logged jeans.

Of course, you're absolutely right, which is irritating. Not that I don't want you to be right, but the starkness of your letter, putting your finger on such a vital issue with the disarming *I may look like a bumbling idiot at times but here's a stun grenade for you to play with* style with which you write, brings a very real problem into focus. Why indeed do some people experience little or nothing when they express faith in Christ, while others apparently step into the experiential equivalent of an endless firework display?

I confess that I was in the latter category for the first decade or so of my Christian experience. Looking back, I remain convinced that many of the 'happenings' in my life were authentic and heaven-sent. Perhaps I really needed the cascading colours of a few Roman Candles to keep me going; completely green behind the ears when it came to anything spiritual, I was grateful for the days when the air seemed to crackle with the activity of God. Of course that doesn't solve the problem for others who have the same or even a greater need for the assurance that comes when there's a sense that God's at work, and yet, for them, all that happens is that nothing happens.

But some of my 'experiences', frankly, were not created by divine or angelic activity, but were simply the fruit of bad teaching. Let me proffer some examples.

I was given some dreadful advice about the significance of the Bible. A well-meaning friend gave me a bit of 'wisdom', which turned out to be as useful as a strychnine tablet. He said that if I needed to hear the voice of God about a specific decision I was wrestling with, whatever portion of Scripture I was currently reading would address that situation. If I were to present this idea on a flip chart it would look something like this:

1. Adrian and Bridget are prayerfully considering moving to a new part of the country, possibly Hull.

2. Adrian is currently reading Jonah. Jonah is told to go somewhere else, not, as it turns out, Hull, but Nineveh. Adrian wonders if Nineveh means 'Hull' in ancient Assyrian, or whether it's enough to go somewhere else simply because he's reading that Jonah was told to go somewhere else. Bridget is reading Ephesians, which has no mention of docks, cod, flat caps or mushy peas, and is therefore quite unhelpful.

3. Adrian is then confused because Jonah doesn't want to go to Nineveh, and indeed heads in the opposite direction, so much does he hate Nineveh, whereas Adrian and Bridget rather like Hull, especially that little chip shop down by the pier that does excellent locally produced steak and kidney pies.

4. Adrian is further confused by Jonah's riding in a ship, because when the storm comes, the reluctant prophet finds himself thrown overboard and staring at the underside of the ship's *hull*. Does this mean that all roads lead to Hull?

If the above seems absurd, then let me confess with scarlet-faced embarrassment that I've had a few of these internal mental dialogues. Of course, it takes about a millisecond to see just how implausible this ridiculous notion is; if I'm praying about my vocation and I happen to be reading through the Song of Solomon, I might find all that talk of dripping pomegranates mildly thrilling, but not terribly applicable to that specific decision. Likewise, while I'm sure that the explicit directions about sheep slaughtering found in Leviticus are enthralling for some, it's hardly going to provide direction for a vegetarian who is considering overseas service.

As it turns out, I got myself in a terrible mess because of this quack advice.

It nearly cost me my marriage. I'd met Kay, who was a delightful, Christianly keen teenager. Finding that I rather liked her, I then heard yet another gospel old wives' tale – this time that there was only one person on planet Earth that was God's choice for me, another bad idea that is terrifying enough to drive any sensible soul to celibacy, for fear that the wrong choice might be made. I began to pray about this relationship and was hoping that God might have something to say about it. Unfortunately I was reading through the book of Proverbs at the time, which has a few stern warnings about the perils of hanging out with prostitutes. I am mortified to confess it, but for a while I was genuinely fearful. If this was God speaking into my specific situation through the Scripture that I was reading at the time, did this mean that Kay actually was not the innocent bright young Christian thing that I thought she was? Was she actually engaging in a bit of entrepreneurial but immoral activity, that was a nice little earner on the side but hardly appropriate if she was to become a minister's wife? You see, some of my 'experiences' weren't really experiences involving God at all, but rather came because I put two and two together and made forty-six.

Then there was the problem that I had with baptising everything with significance. This was the result of my *mishearing* some advice given to me. Someone suggested that the whole of life is the sphere of our learning as Christian disciples: nothing wrong with that. But I managed to get that twisted around into *everything that happens is planned by God to teach you something*. So, if Sainsbury's runs out of fish fingers, the cricket gets rained off, the cat coughs and gets flu, or England lose on penalties (a truly everyday experience) then God was not only trying to tell me something through these minor happenings, but had choreographed them in order to nudge me into learning. Conversely, bad things that happened (even minor irritations, like gravy spillage) suggested spiritual warfare. Therefore, when I ran out of petrol, I wondered what the Lord was trying to tell me through it, and speculated that perhaps Satan was camping in my bathroom, or worse, making use of a siphon. I now know, of course, what the Lord was saying as my empty engine petered out on the hard shoulder of the motorway: 'Fill thine tank, idiot one.' When everything that happens has to mean something, some pretty bizarre conclusions will be reached.

My confusion became as thick as pea soup as I imbibed the idea that, whenever God is speaking, there will be coincidental repetition that underscores this. At it's most basic, this means that if I happen to read a particular passage of Scripture in my daily Bible reading notes, and then that passage is mentioned during the Sunday morning sermon, and then again, coincidently, in the home group meeting the following Wednesday, that this therefore means that God is broadcasting a message on my wavelength and I'd better take notice.

So now I was bouncing like a pinball between out of context Scriptures and ordinary happenings laminated with significance, and if I bumped into the same Scripture more than a couple of times in as many days, I wondered what HQ was saying to me.

There was a fourth confusion to come. You mentioned speaking in tongues.

It happened to me. I did (and I still do) believe that the Bible celebrates speaking in tongues as a valid experience for today. I'm just not sure that what happened to me was that. I sat in a room with others being prayed for, listening to people murmuring what sounded like a list of the Sri Lankan cricket team (I've laughed until I've cried over the piece that you did on that), and then feeling conspicuously like Yogi Bear (he of yabba dabba do fame), I muttered a few words which, in my case, sounded like the ingredients of a Madhur Jaffrey Chicken Pasanda: 'Shan-dala Coriander Kurai', which may well have been a deep expression of praise to God, even though it sounded like it needed a mushroom pilau on the side, and perhaps even a naan bread.

And then there was that phase when people went to church primarily to be prayed for and then fall over, hopefully with a catcher waiting in readiness, like a supernatural wicket-keeper. This all gets a bit confusing, because I do know that in the middle of the mess and madness, I *did* meet God and experience something very real and tangible, and I certainly would not want to trifle with that authentic experience. But then there were also times when I fell over and it had nothing to do with God, because I took a dive.

It's awkward when some enthusiastic prayer ministry person is pebble dashing your face with spit, and yelling 'More Lord!!', and nothing is apparently happening. If the person praying is a bit of a spiritual thug (watch out for the ones wearing camouflage trousers and carrying rams' horns) you can end up with your head being pushed so far back that dire spinal damage could be done. Not only that, but the pray-er is looking down the line at his mate, who is knocking people over at speed like skittles at a bowling alley, so he is now feeling bad about himself. The catcher feels useless, and so everyone is made to feel glum by the apparent absence of a Holy Spirit-induced knockout punch.

For times like this I have perfected what I like to describe as the courtesy drop. You check that the wicket-keeper is indeed in place, and at the appropriate moment, simply fall over. You are lowered gently to the ground, where you can take a nap, think about what's for tea or study the socks of the wicket-keepers. Everyone's a winner. The person praying has got a result, the wicket keeper has caught one successfully, and you get left alone for a while. One word of caution is needed, however. People with heart conditions should not try this and indeed should stay away from these gatherings. There would be nothing worse that being knocked over by a massive cardiac arrest only to come round from unconsciousness with a grinning person standing over you yelling 'more Lord', when in fact what you need more of is oxygen and, possibly, a defibrillator.

In short, Adrian, quite a few of those 'carpet times' had little to do with God.

Permit me one further confession of confusion. I also wandered into the minefield of believing that my feelings were a solid indicator that God was with me. I was told that the crowning confirmation that should be in place before any major decision was made is *peace*. The 'biblical' backup for this idea is to be found in Colossians 3:15: 'Let the peace of Christ rule your hearts.' Peace is like an umpire at a cricket match, they said. To proceed without a prevailing sense of peace in my heart would be violating that principle: in the end, my emotional calm was what called the final shot. How I felt was the ultimate referee.

What a disaster that was. I was utterly dismayed at the thought that I might take a wrong decision and perhaps miss out on marrying the one and only unique person in the cosmos that God had selected for me, who might be a mustachioed Christian goat-herd called Brawn Hilda living on the windswept hills of Estonia. If I messed up, not only would I be condemned to a 'second choice' marriage, but poor old Brawn Hilda would be consigned to a dull life watching goats swanning around (maybe that should be goating around) and reading Leviticus for slaughtering tips, her only joy the sight of her country occasionally winning the Eurovision Song Contest.

I felt more fear than peace, and because I didn't have peace, I didn't have peace, if you get my drift, Adrian. It never occurred to me to look at the context for Colossians 3; Paul was writing to his pals about church unity, and calling upon them to allow peace to win the day in their conflicts; the verse has got nothing to do with subjective guidance whatsoever. But because I couldn't get peace, I felt more turbulence, until I felt like chucking the whole thing in or checking myself into a secure facility.

Helpfully, someone came along who nudged me out of that mad zone. That would be you.

Yes, you, Adrian Vivian Eldad Plass (I bet not many people know about your little middle name secret, eh Adrian?) You told me, either in person or in one of your nine hundred books, that my emotions are *not* the barometer of my spirituality.

So some of my experiences were definitely questionable, some were suspect, and a few hold firm as I look back. What is both a relief and a worry, Adrian, is that those epic God encounters don't tend to happen to me much any more. I know that having committed the last sentence to ink that there will be some readers who will rush to conclude that I am spiritually dead or worse. Is it because I've realised that to look at these 'experiences' with a more critical eye is not only my privilege, but also my responsibility? I don't want to lock God up in a deist box, and make him the Creator of the Universe who has now gone away on an extended vacation. God *does* intervene, and it is possible that at times he does so but we simply don't notice.

But it might be that some of us have an inordinate hunger for happenings.

Earlier we mentioned Elijah, one of my favourite Bible characters. He certainly had a few landmark moments in his life. I've never called down fire from heaven (and have presided at a few soggy barbecues); I've not performed a food multiplication miracle, organised a drought, or raised someone from the dead (although waking teenagers up in the morning for school required almost as much faith). When he was at his wit's end, holed up in the cave humming '*We shall not, we shall not be moved*,' God allowed something that God wasn't in. Sounds strange, doesn't it?

The Bible records that a great powerful rock-shattering wind whipped up, *but the Lord was not in the wind*. An earthquake rumbled (threatening to cave in the cave where the hapless Elijah was parked, clamped to his own hopelessness), *but the Lord was not in the earthquake*. And then a third spectacular happening: fire, a reminder of the Carmel showdown, *but the Lord was not in the fire*.

And then . . .

There was the sound of a still small voice. The best translation might be 'the sound of gentle silence' or 'the silent sound'. I ask this as a question, not as a proposition: is it just possible that Elijah could have become a sign addict, hungry for happenings, and now God was leading him to a place where he could do faith in the relative silence?

Because that's where most, if not all of us do faith. Tom Cruise might hear backing music when he kisses his wife in a movie, but you and I aren't being followed around by an orchestra.

And then, perhaps every now and again, the silence is broken. Something strange happens – an answer to prayer comes. It's strange, because it's rather odd that God should show any interest in the lives of those of us who live in the affluent West when most of the world will tuck themselves up with empty bellies tonight. But he does. And it's wonderful when he does. But much of faith is about living hopefully in the relative quietness.

Perhaps we should stop trying to think there is such a thing as a normative experience for the Christian disciple. I've struggled with that idea ever since I read Watchman Nee's classic book *The Normal Christian Life* (I think that his parents, who dubbed him 'Watchman' should have read the more relevant tome, *The Normal Christian Name*). What's normal? Every marriage, friendship, working relationship is unique.

Perhaps we should stop tormenting ourselves with comparisons. And if that seems terse, consider the advice given by Jesus to Peter over breakfast. Having been told that he would die a martyr's death, Peter is understandably concerned to know what's going to happen to John (who is repeatedly dubbed '*the disciple whom Jesus loved*' in John's gospel, which, irritatingly, he wrote). Perhaps Peter was worried that he was going to end up in the New Testament equivalent of Alcatraz while favourite John retired to a beach house in Hawaii.

But Jesus gave short shrift to the question: '. . . what is that to you? You must follow me' (John 21:22). Questions are the stuff of faith. And yet trust is demanded when God gently informs us that he is currently not making an answer available, and that we need to instead get on with the business of keeping in step with him today. It doesn't fix everything, and frankly, I don't like it, but perhaps it's true.

By the way, before I sign off, I should make two confessions. First, I know that Watchman Nee's first name was not actually *Watchman*, and that his parents didn't actually dub him that. It was probably Brian, or Ron, or, being Chinese, *Yikitakkkeishisma*, so Watchman rolls off the tongue a little more easily. And the second confession is about your middle names, Adrian. How silly of me to suggest that your full designation is *Adrian Vivian Eldad* (Plass). I made that up. What is your real middle name?

Lots of love,
Jeffrey Brenda Lucas

TWENTY-ONE

Dear Jeff,

I've been looking back over your last couple of letters and chewing over my responses to some of the things that you said. One response is ridiculously inappropriate. It just occurred to me that the words used by the cleaning lady who discovered you naked in the sitting room of your chalet could possibly have been an obscure sexual code. Who knows what might have happened if you had winked suggestively, used a couple of air quotes and replied, 'Yes, I would just love you to *hoover my carpet.*' However, let's not go down there. Oh dear, no, sorry, that's definitely a metaphor too far . . .

From the ridiculous to the sublime, in an earlier letter I briefly referred to your account of staging a burglary at the age of eight in order to fill the vacuum of power and significance in your life, but I want to say how stirred I have been by that story. It reminded me of one or two incidents in my own childhood, but it also stirs up memories of the children Bridget and I encountered in a variety of residential establishments during the first phase of our working lives, many of whom were exhibiting behavioural problems for very similar reasons. These boys and girls, ranging from eleven to eighteen years old, could be sad, mad, bad or a mixture of all three. Some had only been sent away from home because their parents had screwed everything up, others would undoubtedly have been categorised as autistic nowadays. A very few were just plain mean. A small proportion shouldn't have been there at all. We became fond of lots of our charges.

A thing that many of these kids had in common was a dimension of puzzlement and confusion. In his parable of the sower, Jesus said that some of the seed fell on rocky places where there was not much soil, so that it grew up quickly in the shallow earth. But the plants withered and died when the sun came up because they had no root. This was exactly the problem for a large proportion of the children that we worked with. The strong roots of love, affirmation and consistent care simply were not there. Before trying to plant any seeds in the wasteland of their souls, it was necessary to break up this hard ground and cultivate a new depth of rich soil capable of nourishing green shoots of self-worth, optimism and a belief in the possibility of love.

And we are not talking about some airy-fairy, pseudo-spiritual thing here. God knows we encountered enough of that nonsense over the years. Occasionally Christian individuals or groups practising the Mike Tyson model of evangelism would erupt onto the scene and persuade a child or a group of children to ask Jesus into their lives. From the point of view of these kids, it was a no-brainer. You said the prayer, or whatever was asked of you, and then, according to the shiny-eyed ones, sin would be overcome in your life and the brilliant times would begin. Except that they didn't, because the bringers of the word had cleared off rejoicing mightily, and the new convertees woke up next morning to find that nothing had changed and the stony ground was as parched and impenetrable as ever.

A girl that Bridget worked with in an approved school in the West Country was promised by a minister that if she read her Bible every day and became a good Christian, he and his wife would take her to live in their home. Each evening she doggedly read a bit of the Bible he had left with her, and greeted interruptions with a snarled obscenity, followed by the immortal words, 'I'm getting religious.' The church marches on, eh, Jeff?

Naturally a lot of these children were puzzled and confused. How could they not be when love was just an unsubstantiated rumour?

No, the process of reconstitution and genuine change can take years, and more often than not involves the faithful, persistent support of people who genuinely care about these damaged hearts and souls, beloved of God, who have heard the Spirit call but are not equipped to make the journey on their own. Bridget and I became particularly attached to a boy whose background was so desperately hopeless that it was hard to see the prospect of anything positive happening in his future. We had a great deal of involvement in his life over the years, but the process of supporting him was grindingly frustrating and discouraging. He had become a Christian (whatever God decides that actually means), and it really was important to him, but I can recall silently and (in suitable environments) not so silently screaming at God:

'Well, come on, then! Do something! Change him. Fiddle with his inner workings. Take a divine screwdriver and adjust his controls. Turn him into a sausage-sizzling, chorus-singing, clear-eyed child of God. You're the one who does the miracles. What are you waiting for? What are you actually giving him?'

Only recently did we begin to understand that, as far as we were concerned and needed to know, one of the very concrete things that God had given this awkward prodigal was, quite simply, us. We are part of a support system that has enabled him to survive and even flourish in some areas of his life.

Not very promising on the face of it but, inadequate as Bridget and I undoubtedly were and are, we were the ones chosen to be Jesus for this lad. We may be twits of the first order, but twits is all God has got in this world, a not particularly extensive twit pool to choose from. And we happened to be nearest at the time.

Coincidentally, in the same week that I read about your fake burglary we received an email from a man we had known as a teenager many years ago when we worked in what was then rather hideously known as a School for Maladjusted Boys. This chap's communication was positive communication in many ways, but between the lines we seemed to detect that same sense of hurt, tentative mystification. Why had he been sent away to that place all those years ago? Who made the decision that he was the sort of boy who belonged in a community of emotional evacuees that included the delinquent, the deluded and the desperate? Who on earth could that unhappy child have been, the one who couldn't for the life of him work out what was going on, or why no one ever really bothered to answer the questions that he hardly dared put into words?

I was never one of those kids in a residential establishment, Jeff, but I know the feeling. So, I would guess, do you. Who was that little boy who, with a burning ball of trouble inside, turned his house upside-down so that he could prove that he was something more than a faint silhouette of himself? And has anyone ever been back to explain to him exactly what was happening on that strange, wonderful, dreadful day when the worst could

have happened and all he received was kindness? I hope
so.

When I was working with children in care, I wrote
these little verses.

Stranded in the hall of mirrors
I will struggle to avoid
Images that cannot show me
Something long ago destroyed

In the darkness, in the distance
In a corner of my mind
Stands a puzzled child in silence
Lonely, lost and far behind

In imagination only
In my single mirror see
Clear and calm, the one reflection
Of the person that is me.

That, in my view, is what God is doing for so many men,
women and children, human beings who passionately
long for a clear and uncluttered reflection of themselves
in the still pool of his love. And maybe the complexity of
that yearning offers an answer to all our written and spoken and unspoken questions about authenticity and con-
sistency in the way that we experience the presence of
God. It can be him directly. It can be other people. It can
take three seconds. It can take ninety years. It can be
simple. It can be unbelievably complicated. It can require
enormous courage. It can demand excruciating submis-
sion. It can involve impossible forgiveness. It can present
us with the demoralising, silver-lined cloud that is the
painful joy of being forgiven. How could we ever have

convinced ourselves that the practical, bespoke love of God could be contained within a book of cowboy songs and three or four ludicrously simplistic principles? Are we mad?

I suspect I might be mad, but I know for sure I'm tired, Jeff. I'm going to take the dog for a walk. Look forward to hearing from you soon.

Much love,
Adrian

TWENTY-TWO

Dear Jeff,

While waiting for your next letter, I've been asking myself what people would think if they ever got to read this correspondence of ours. They wouldn't be at all surprised by the funny stories, would they? You and I are incurably anecdotal and seriously addicted to the ridiculous. In fact, as a writer I can never truly relax until I am comfortably launched into a narrative of some kind. It's a bit of a weakness, I suppose. Writing in any other way is hard work for me. Readers might be quite surprised, though, to discover the depth of angst and agony that accompanies our respective journeys with Jesus. There is so much to react to and against in Christian experience, sometimes with laughter, sometimes with anger, sometimes with pain and sorrow, sometimes with love and appreciation, and quite often with total bewilderment. Nowadays I find it much easier and probably more helpful to be truthful about the negative elements on this list. The same might apply to you. Having said that, I would be very sad if our phantom reader was so distracted by the humour and the hand-wringing that they failed to collide with the positive passion that inhabits and fuels our desire to be part of making Jesus visible in the world.

This morning I asked myself the following question. How does being a follower of Jesus practically affect the way that I live in this world? The answer, I am overwhelmingly pleased to say, involves a story.

It's not much of a story really, but I think it makes the point.

I was at a large Christian event a few years ago (somewhere in the northern hemisphere if you want to narrow down the exact location, or it might have been the southern, one or the other, anyway), and I was in a seriously negative mood. I sort of enjoy some of these big religious jamborees, but quite a lot of them turn me into a glowering pile of muttering, critical misery. Sitting, arms folded, on a ridiculously small chair in the half darkness at the side of the stage on this occasion, waiting for my turn to go on, and reflecting glumly on a day that had already been long and tiring, I began to find just about everything annoying.

For a start there was the general neurotically positive ethos that commonly pervades these bashes. Every person taking part in the presentation seemed magically transfigured by the ascent of three steps at the side of the stage. To my jaundiced eye there was something irritatingly brittle about the effulgent joy, assurance and beaming goodwill with which they addressed the audience or congregation or whatever we've decided is the right and godly thing to call them.

Then there was the worship band, and especially the member of it nearest me, a wilting youth shaped like an anorexic banana whose guitar was slung just above his simian knees. As spokesman for the band, he had one or two incoherent things to mumble through his weeping willow hairstyle in the direction of the congregation/audience before obliging everybody to get involved in yet another impenetrable wall of noise. Years ago I invented an excruciating Christian youth band called Bad News For The Devil whose music suggested a piano falling through a lift-shaft. This crowd would have made them sound like the Royal Philharmonic. They made my head ache.

Almost as bad was the man who padded on up a little later with his acoustic guitar to sing a song given to him by God. I've made too many jokes about that sort of claim in the past, so I won't bother now. Suffice it to say that the rhymes in his lyrics were as unsuited as victims of arranged marriages between beings from different solar systems, and his highest notes sounded like a dehydrated bloodhound trapped in rubble. When, I asked myself, did we make this fateful decision that orthodox worthiness is a reasonable substitute for quality? He eventually left the stage, having preached a heel-bouncing mini-sermon and done a second song when he wasn't supposed to, so palpably moved by his own presentation that he barely registered the dull restlessness of the audience/congregation.

By the time it was my turn to go on stage, I was in a black mood. In what sense did I belong here? What was the point of it? Why did we all continue to shore up this tottering edifice of Toy Town evangelicalism when its manifestations were so twitteringly shallow? I delivered my stuff as well as I could, then crept away as quickly as possible, returning to my hotel to eat cheese and pickle sandwiches in bed and watch rubbish on television until it was time to go to sleep.

When I woke in the morning I didn't feel very pleased with myself. Sitting there, distractedly brushing crumbs from the cover of my bed, I asked myself who on earth I thought I was. Those people up on that stage last night were only performing and behaving according to their lights. Who was I to judge them? If I had been able to sit there last night feeling so cynical and negative what were the actual manifestations of my so-called Christianity? I went down to breakfast with only one strong and confident belief lodged in my soul. I needed hot, strong coffee.

I got some, but breakfast was really busy in the hotel that morning, and there seemed to be only two people doing all the work. One of them, an East European judging by her accent, can only have been twenty or so, an attractive girl wearing a black headband to keep her flying hair under control. She was racing around the breakfast area collecting plates, serving meals, clearing and wiping tables and meeting questions or complaints with determined good humour. I noticed, though, that once or twice when she passed through a pair of swing doors into the kitchen area, the expression on her face drooped and clouded with weariness.

The other hotel employee was an older, stoutish man of Asian extraction whose main task seemed to be ensuring that containers of orange juice and milk, cold foods and bread for toasting were continually topped up in readiness for newly arriving guests. This nervous, friendly chap was working with as much energy and commitment as his colleague. Every now and then the two of them would collide in the midst of their toils and enjoy a hurried confabulation before hurrying off to tackle the next job.

I was one of the last to leave the dining-room. As I headed for the exit, I found myself wondering if anyone was going to thank these two people for the cheerful, industrious way in which they'd served us. They were paid for working at the hotel, of course, but probably not very much. A little gratitude, that was what they needed and deserved. Stopping by the counter next to the door, I addressed my breakfast team as they cleaned and tidied their service area.

'You've worked really hard, haven't you?'

It was like switching on two light bulbs. Such smiles and nods and sighs. They both started talking at the same time.

'Oh, yes, it has been hard this morning because . . .

'We are short staffed, you see, and so . . .'

'. . . there was only us and so we had to . . .'

'. . . the two of us had to do everything. It has been hard work, but . . .'

'We have finished now and everyone had a good breakfast, I think . . .'

They ran out of breath.

'Well, thank you very, very much for working so hard, and for looking after your guests so well. Good morning.'

'Good morning, sir, and thank you for . . .'

'Yes, thank you, and have a very good day, sir.'

That's what happened at breakfast. Something else happened an hour later, while I was sitting on a platform, waiting for my train at the nearest railway station.

I knew that if the trains behaved themselves I could just about make an event later in the day to which Bridget and I had been invited. I knew how very important it was to the person who had invited us that Bridget and I should both be there. I also knew that no one, not our host, nor Bridget nor anyone else would blame me if I didn't turn up. After all, I was coming back after a busy day yesterday, and everyone knows how awkward trains can be. You can always fog the details a bit when it comes to journeys that involve two or three changes. When I met the person concerned in a couple of days I would just sigh and click my tongue and spread my arms and take both of his hands in mine and express regret and that would be that. I leaned back in my seat, closed my eyes and tried to relax.

I made the event with fifteen minutes to spare.

So what, you will be asking yourself, Jeff, has all this got to do with anything? Well, I suppose it's a bit like when your kids are teenagers and someone else's mother or father comments on how polite and thoughtful your child was in their house, and you nearly fall over with shock but desperately try to look as though that's how they behave at home as well. In one sense I doubt if God was too troubled by me mumbling and grumbling all on my own at the side of that stage, but he would be (and I'm sure sometimes has been) very angry and disappointed if I fail to represent his love and grace to the people with whom I actually come in contact. If there is one thing I think I might have learned about God it is that, as far as he is concerned, there is not a single unimportant person in the world, and we (Lord help us!) are his means of meeting them and conveying the unexpected truth that they are, to quote a previous letter, 'not alone'. Those two people in the hotel dining room and the friend who so wanted me to be at his very special event didn't just need me, they needed God in me. It's enough, Jeff. As I think I have already mentioned, I don't mind delivering the post for God, even if I do mutter under my breath as I trudge up the front garden path.

God bless, Jeff,
Adrian

PS: I'm even more glad that no one will have access to our correspondence after writing this letter. Anorexic banana? The culture in our family and among our closest friends excludes all that 'being hurt and taking deep offence' stuff. My wife suffered from anorexia when she was a teenager, but she would never take flippant references to this horrible complaint personally.

In this connection, I read in some magazine recently that a reader had been 'hurt and deeply offended' by an article that made reference to 'brainstorming', the practice of throwing random ideas together as a first step towards solving a problem or completing a task. 'Brainstorming' is also a term used (insensitively and inappropriately) in connection with epilepsy, a condition endured for many years by one of my closest friends. Well, coincidentally, Jeff, I have decided to be personally hurt and deeply offended by any attempt to dictate which words I should use as long as I use them in the right context, so there – with elaborately decorated knobs on.

Having said all that, I shall not be unhappy to avoid the many letters of complaint that I would be likely to receive from anorexia sufferers, members of the Royal Society for the Prevention of Cruelty to Bananas, the Anorexic Banana Foundation, the Musicians Union, the Society for the Protection of Anorexic Musicians Shaped Like Bananas, Friends of Curved Fruit, Friends of Anorexic Curved Fruit, Friends of Bent Musicians (that one probably does exist, and should if it doesn't), Pointless Peeling Causes Pain International etc. etc.

I must go. I seem to be spiralling down into insanity, and I would like to make it clear that I am using that word in a responsible and caring way.

> Yours,
> Adrian

TWENTY-THREE

Dear Adrian,

Great to hear from you. I think that, in asking how being followers of Jesus should change the way we live in the world, you've answered your own question. The wisdom to which I referred was all wrapped up in the dynamite statement that one could easily dismiss as being a line from the musical *Annie* or something that one might find in a Disney magazine; it's so simple, it can sound trite. Here's the statement, in case you're wondering: *there are no unimportant people in the world.*

If somehow we could get our heads and hearts around that little gem, then surely the world wouldn't quite know what had hit it. It means that the vast majority of the world's population of middle ground, even mediocre souls matter desperately, and are worthy of attention and kindness. It also means that the celebrity-culture myth of the extraordinary and ultra beautiful needs to be shredded. A soul is no more worthy if they are blessed with high cheekbones and large, perfectly shaped breasts (if you're female), or if they have an expensive media machine that can pump out endless trivia about them to those sad enough to be interested, or even if they are blessed with special talent. As I've reviewed our letters, it seems that small actions – a caring word, a waitress working hard, being prepared to listen – all of these everyday and profoundly ordinary actions are actually the rich gravy on the meal that is life.

And that is why I sometimes find myself joining you with a nervous feeling at those large Christian events, where everyone is being told to do and be something epic. But not everyone can be a campaigner, a politician, a crusader on their local council, a gifted counsellor in their local church, or a theologian who can help us swim with confidence in unfathomable mysteries. Most of us are just . . . ordinary. Sometimes there can be a push to break out of obscurity and be an epic world changer, but chaps like Wilberforce are actually quite rare.

I'd like to push that thought a little further, and suggest that there's great liberation in knowing what we can't do. *Britain's Got Talent* is one of those television shows that surfs on the tantalising message: you can be different. Greatness, whatever it is can be yours. In doing so, perhaps it exploits.

As frumpy Susan Boyle burst into a song from *Les Miserables* and then checked into the Priory feeling miserable, we wondered whether *Britain's Got Talent* meant that *Britain's Got Tacky*. Were cheeky chappies Ant and Dec the grinning hosts of some innocent family entertainment, or the masters of ceremony at the modern equivalent of a public hanging? The debate intensified when a junior competitor punctuated their performance with tears.

Whatever our conclusion, the one hundred million Internet hits for Ms Boyle's *YouTube* performance show that we're intrigued by talent unearthed from an unexpected source. The jeering crowd who sneered at Susan before she opened her mouth was wrong, to our delight. Simon Cowell's dentally enhanced mouth fell open with shock as the ugly duckling sang like a nightingale. The judges thought she couldn't, and she could.

Christianity creates a can-do culture of aspiration. The Bible is loaded with stories of rejects, plucked from obscurity by God, who did remarkable things that far outshine fifteen minutes of fame in the celebrity thunderdome. Jesus' choosing a motley crew of unlikely lads and ladies to change the world says this: we can become other than what we are. We are not sentenced to sameness, but can expand our horizons, grow and change. The parable speaks to all of us, not a selected few: *You've got talents, now use them.* Of course, in Jesus' day, a talent was a unit of money. But the message is still clear: whatever your abilities, use them well.

But is there a need to add a word of caution? Some of us are good at discovering our gifts. But are we as willing to honestly face our limits? I had a difficult conversation once with a man who insisted that he had a divinely-given ability to sing. He spent lots of time composing songs, downloaded, he insisted, from the God of the Universe who was giving him melodies and lyrics. Those who listened endured a noise not unlike that of a chicken being strangled, and concluded that if God was giving this wannabe Pavarotti songs, then it was probably because he didn't want them.

When gently confronted with the news that listening to his singing was as pleasant as hearing a fire alarm, he was indignant. *You can't* sounded like blasphemy to him. 'But I can do all things through Christ who strengthens me', he spluttered, completely wrenching prisoner Paul's words out of context. He cannot fly (without wings or a ticket), perform brain surgery, or (being male), give birth. He can huff and puff and believe that by faith he can blow a house down, but the fact is he can't.

Recognising our horizons is a step towards content-
ment, and enables us to recognise the God-given gifts that
we *do* enjoy. If we don't learn to say *I can't*, then we risk
spending our whole lives never getting around to doing
what we can; we're too busy hoping and dreaming for
what will never be.

And so I know that I am not equipped to communicate
with small children. Asked to speak to a group of
American three-year-olds, I launched into a lecture about
the two house parliamentary system that we enjoy in
Britain. The bewildered tots looked mildly terrified. One
of them actually started to cry, and I don't think she was
lamenting the injustices of politically awarded peerages
or the misuse of expenses in the Commons. She was
frightened by the strange man. Me.

That's why I don't try to do much DIY any more. For
years I ignored the fearful intercessory screaming of my
family when I tried to build shelves, wire a plug or fix
anything that was broken. But it's no good. To say *I can't*
can be liberating.

So now, as I write this, how glad I am for the electrician
who is fitting the ceiling fan in my study. This means that
I will not fall off a ladder, electrocute myself, swear copiously, wire the fan backwards, or end up getting caught
on the blades.

And I'm cool with that. Literally.

>   With love to you,
>   Jeff

TWENTY-FOUR

Dear Jeff,

I'm so relieved to learn that for you, as for me, the 'D' in DIY stands for 'Delegate'. In the past I have felt so intimidated by people who are experts at making and mending and building and converting and decorating. You know the sort of thing I mean. They show you round their house, indicating with all manner of extravagant technical mimes the miracles they have wrought since moving in.

'What we've done,' they explain with irritatingly calm absorption, 'is to take the upper floor of the house and simply switch it round with the lower. See what I mean? Did it in a couple of days with a friend. Then this week the wife and I have been rotating the walls by ninety degrees so that the building faces south instead of east. Puts the value up by at least fifty thousand. All you need for a job like that is some RSJs, a few lengths of two by four and a ribbing tool. Next month we're going to rip out all the internal walls, give the place a lick of paint and build a quarter-sized replica of the Alamo right inside the house so that Jean can start doing B&B for Americans on holiday.'

Hmm. I changed a plug once. A tour round my house would be less than impressive.

'What we've done here,' I would explain, indicating an unpleasant stain running down the wallpaper beside a window, 'is to completely ignore the fact that for some time water's been coming through when it rains. That way, you see, we can hope that somehow the problem will go away without anything being done about it. And then, in a couple of months we're planning to panic and spend a ridiculous amount of money getting some dodgy builder to pretend he's fixed it, when we could have done it ourselves for next to nothing just after it started. That's the intention, anyway . . .'

No, my attitude to these things has changed. Nowadays I get the dodgy builder in as soon as I spot the problem.

I guess it's all about facing your limitations so that you are primed, both to work and live within them, and to accept that there will be occasions when God scarily and supernaturally makes it possible for horizon-busting miracles to happen. You mentioned in a previous letter, Jeff, the need to take responsibility for the obvious, whatever God decides to do about the rest. What was the Lord's message for you when you ran out of petrol on the motorway: 'Fill thine tank, idiot,' wasn't it? I thought of that the other day when I came across a copy of a memorable old Gracie Fields music hall song. When I was at teacher training college we used it in a radio documentary about Jack the Ripper. Let me share it with you. It'll never make the Anglican Hymnal, but it's a great song.

Heaven will protect an honest gel,
An an-gi-el will guard you, little Nell.
When these rich men tempt you, Nelly,
With their spark-el-ling Moselly,
Say "Nay! nay!" and do be very care-fu-el!

And if some old bloated blasé roué swell
'I'll kiss you, we're alone in this hotel;'
Breathe a prayer he shall not do it
And then biff him with the cruet,
Then Heaven will protect an honest gel![6]

I may be wrong (was that a rumble of thunder I just heard in the distance?) but I suspect there are times when Jesus himself, if consulted, would say:

'Well, yes, turning the other cheek and earnest prayer are definitely preferred options, but certain situations do call for additional, more practical solutions. Putting petrol in cars that will stop moving if you don't is one example, and prayer accompanied by the odd carefully aimed biff with a cruet could just occasionally be another. Perhaps biffing greed and poverty and sickness and injustice with some sort of metaphorical cruet wouldn't be such a bad idea – don't quote me, though, for goodness sake!'

I wonder if God gets fed up with being quoted, Jeff. I think I would if I was him. How many times in the last two thousand years has the Bible been used to misrepresent the nature and the will and the creative initiatives of God? We've all done it, of course. I certainly have. In fact, I dread to think how often my own interpretation of verses, or misconceptions about the versatility of the Holy Spirit have steered people away from Jesus rather than towards him. It must drive him mad. Well, we know it does.

When the disciples officiously turned away a bunch of children who were trying to get close to that brilliant man who told lots of stories and kept magicking people better there was no doubt about the Master's response. Seven words recorded in the tenth chapter of Mark's gospel come ringing down the years to remind us how foolish and arrogant it is to suppose that we can ever be totally certain of God's intention in any situation.

'When Jesus saw this he was indignant.'

I believe he still is, often. You might have gathered from our correspondence that it drives me mad when self-appointed guardians of holy law pull out a small, sharply pointed shard of Scripture to stick into the heart of some sad, sinning soul who is not so much an agent of Satan as a child who desperately needs to come to Jesus. There is a Cadfael episode that always used to bring tears to my eyes. The monk is investigating the death of a girl who has given birth out of wedlock and commits suicide after being cruelly repulsed by a priest from whom she has sought absolution.

'She was nothing but a useless whore,' says the priest to Cadfael.

'She was a *child*!' replies Cadfael, his voice laden with indignation and sorrow.

Later that evening the monk quietly visits a corner of unconsecrated ground where the girl is buried and pushes a tiny silver crucifix down into the newly turned soil of her unmarked grave.

There is no doubt about it, law without grace just knocks you down. Grace catches you as you fall and gives you a biscuit – and a job usually.

Of course we all need to be accountable for the things that we do, but years of encountering sinners and being one myself suggests that there is only one true pathway to *what should be* and, as Jesus showed clearly in his encounter with the woman at the well, it runs slap-bang through the middle of *what is*. A couple of examples.

A friend of mine was telling me the other day about going into schools to talk about drugs and alcohol. Faced with a group of teenagers he will first of all ask them to name and describe the very best things about indulgence in these areas. No problem there. This list grows quickly and the items on it are discussed with enthusiasm. He then asks for comments about the worst aspects, and it is here that the real discussion begins. An attractive girl will confess in tears that she only feels pretty when she has been drinking. The others will be amazed to hear this and assure her that she looks lovely all the time. Others will talk worriedly about times when they have felt ashamed of themselves or have feared that they are becoming heavily dependent on artificial stimulants. The exchanges can be surprisingly frank. Most of the work is done by the young people themselves, and the freedom with which they share the truth of these negative elements and look for new answers is largely made possible by my friend's morally neutral acceptance of equally valid truths about the positive effects of drink and drugs.

Similarly, I recall a friend called Rick confessing to me that he had embarked on an adulterous affair with a woman living miles from his home in a town in Wales, a place he visited every month or so in the course of his work. I rather think he expected me to tell him off and spell out 'the rules'. Instead I asked him to tell me what it was about this experience that was enjoyable or powerful enough for him to put a previously happy marriage at risk. It was a bit of a cold start, but he got going after a while. He talked about the sex, the novelty, the delicious secrecy, the making of plans, the rediscovery of what it means to feel attractive.

'Right,' I said mildly, 'so, on the one side you're really enjoying all that, and on the other side you have a marriage that I know you think is worth saving, and a life-long faith that spells out clearly what God thinks about adultery. He doesn't like it, does he? But no one's going to bully you. Not God, certainly not me, not anyone. You have a real choice. You're genuinely free. You can go on with the affair for all the reasons you've just given me, and enjoy every minute of it. Alternatively, you lose the relationship in Wales and recommit yourself to your wife and to God. It's up to you, Rick.'

He shifted uncomfortably in his chair.

'But what would *you* do?'

'Me? I'd make a decision just like you'll have to, but I don't know what it would be. I'm not you. I might go for the Welsh option.'

I took pity on him.

'All right, Rick, I'll tell you honestly what I think. If Jesus was here in the flesh I reckon he'd move over and sit beside you, put his arm round your shoulders and say quite gently, "Rick, I understand how exciting all this has been, but, my friend, you're worth more than this. If you want to help me and join in with what needs to be done in the future you'll have to make the hard decision. I really hope you will, because I love you – and your wife, and I think you know in your heart that this adventure of yours is likely to end in tears. In the end, though, it is up to you."'

What decision did Rick make?

Mind your own business.

One more example which is very small, but was truly helpful to me. It happened at a church we used to attend in the Midlands. There was a fund-raising meal in the church hall one evening, and I was looking forward to it. I like eating, I enjoy talking and I genuinely love listening to what other people have to say – most of the time. Unfortunately I drew what appeared to be the short straw as far as the seating plan was concerned. I was stuck on the end of the table opposite William, a widower from our church who had somehow managed to turn small talk into an art form. He had nothing to say, and he spent an inordinate amount of time saying it. I was so fed up. How would I survive an hour and a half or more of old William rabbiting on endlessly about the shade of stain he was using on his garden fence, or his preference for blankets over 'them newfangled doovay nonsenses'? I thought I was going to die.

Typically, in this sort of situation, the people at the other end of the table seemed to be enjoying a veritable feast of Rabelaisian wit and humour, a feast that was obviously being much enjoyed by the person sitting in the adjacent chair to mine, who had presented her back to me two minutes after the meal began and was likely to stay that way as long as the blasted Wildean set kept up their guffawing and table-rapping and choruses of mirth.

I raged inwardly as my elderly dining companion drivelled on for ten minutes or so about the temperature of his Meals on Wheels, and the size of a new spade recently bought by the man next door. And then, quite suddenly, I felt guilty. Here was I, the one who was always going on about every individual being important, wishing that some dire emergency (an earthquake would have been nice) might relieve me of the burden of pretending to listen to William for another three days or so. I spoke to God in my mind.

'I am sorry,' I said, 'I will do my very best to find William interesting. I'm sure he is really . . .'

'No he's not,' said the other end of the dialogue, 'he's elderly and boring and you'd have to be mad to prefer listening to him instead of being up at the other end of the table. That's not the point.'

'And the point is?'

'Just for me – make old William a gift of your attention for the evening. He's important to me, and you're the one on the spot. That's the job tonight. Take it or leave it.'

I took it. He was still boring, but it was okay.

Jeff, I love the way of Jesus in the world. I love his realism, his affection for the twiddly people, the trust he places in us to keep the grace flowing, his persistence with saints and sinners and the hope he brings to those who are troubled and lost in so many different ways. What a privilege to be part of it all. We're very lucky, you and I, aren't we?

Love and blessings,
Adrian

Endnotes

[1] Williams, R., *Open to Judgement* (London: Dartman Longman and Todd, 1994).

[2] Plass, A., *The Unlocking* (Oxford: BRF, 1995).

[3] Alexander, P., *The Lion Book of Christian Poetry* (Oxford: Lion, 1981).

[4] Lucas, J., *Creating a Prodigal-friendly Church* (London: Zondervan, 2008).

[5] Jerome, J.K., *Three Men in a Boat* (London: Penguin Popular Classics, 2007).

[6] Copyright Francis Day and Hunter, 1933.